Masanao Hirayama
88 Constellations

Masanao Hirayama
88 Constellations

New Documents
Los Angeles

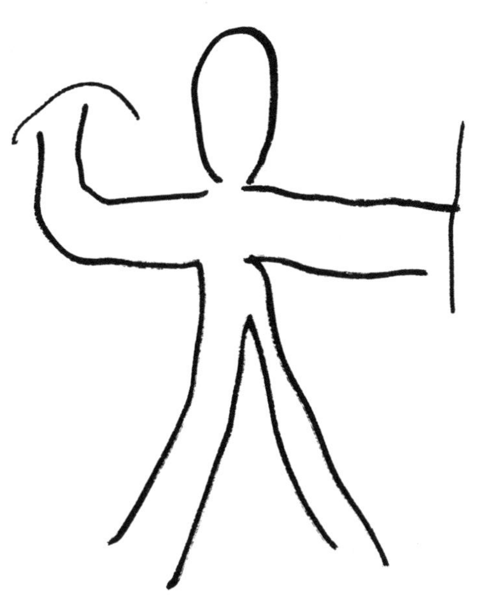

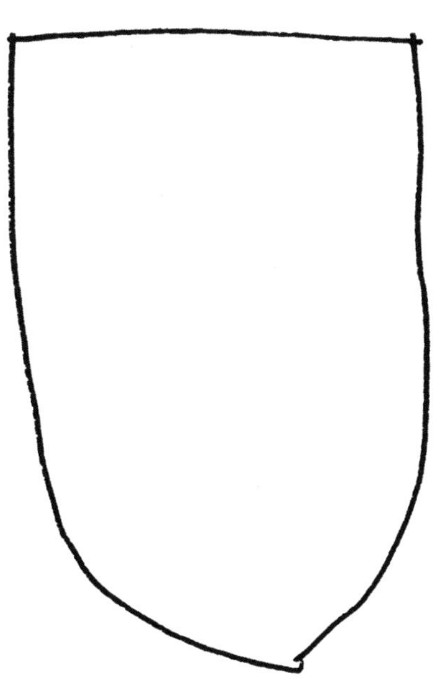

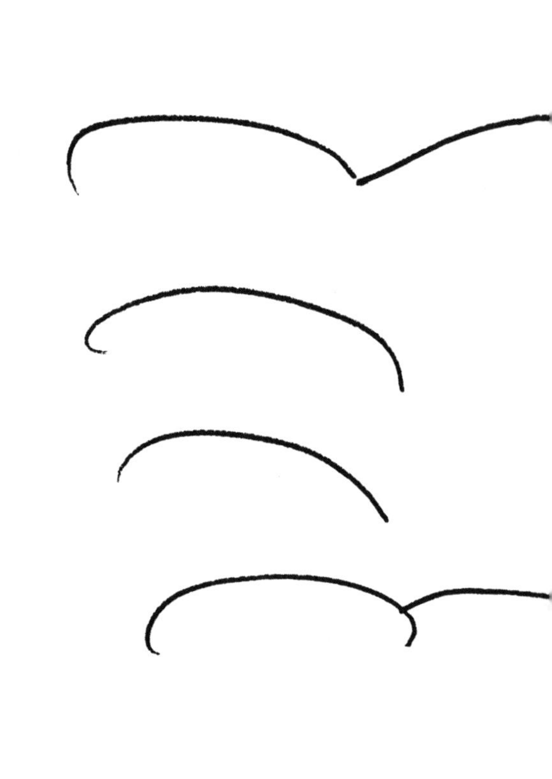

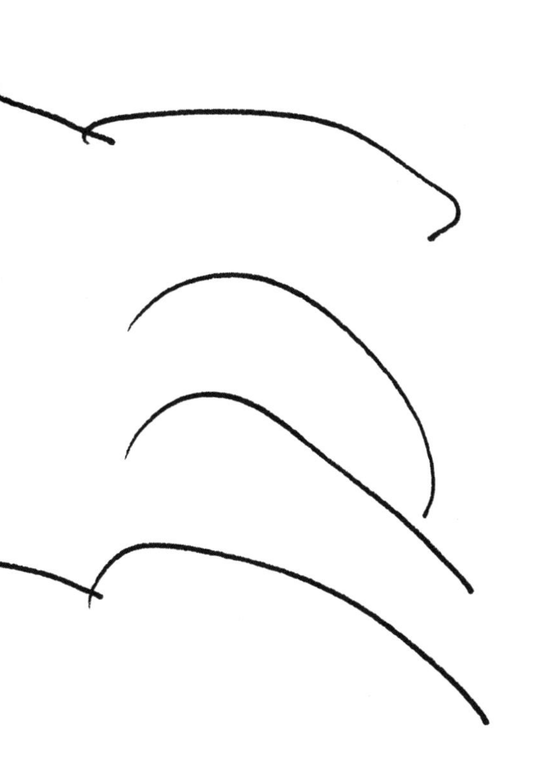

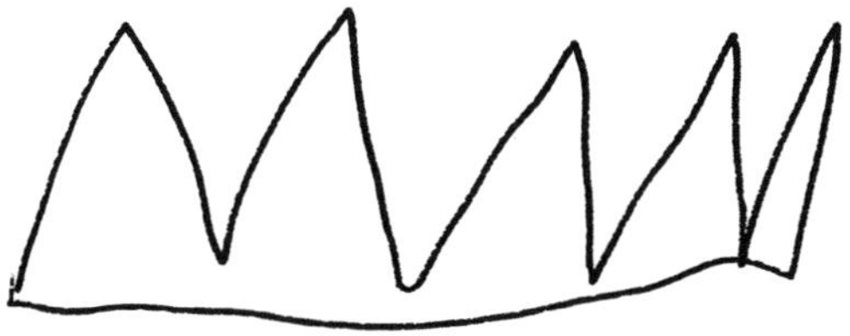

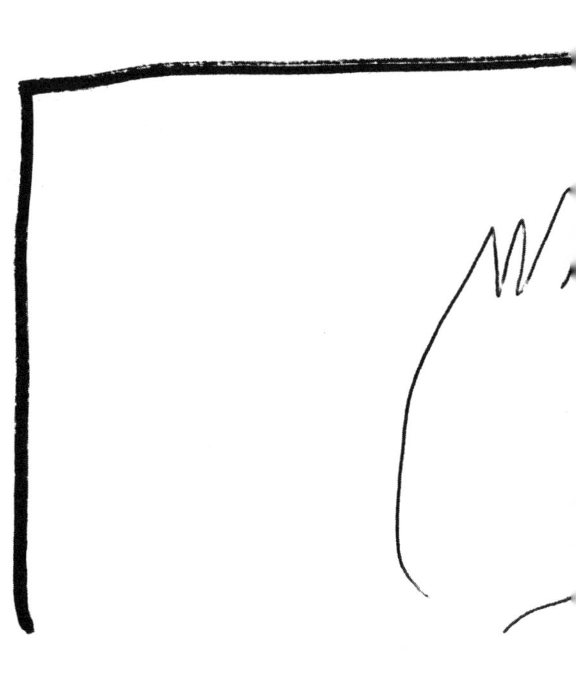

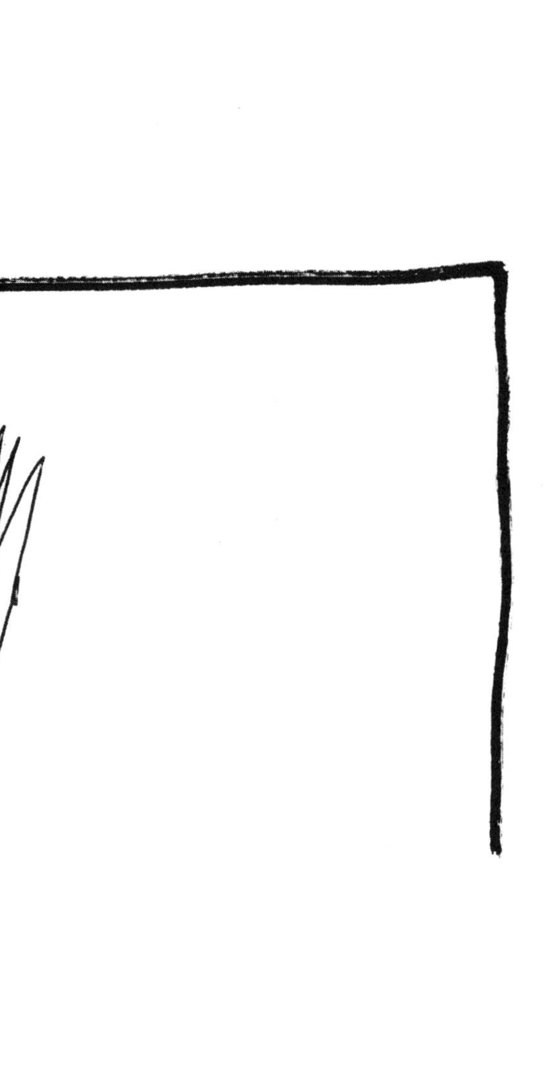

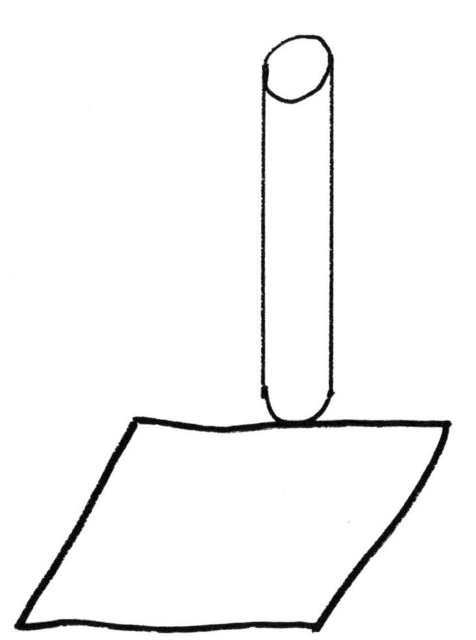

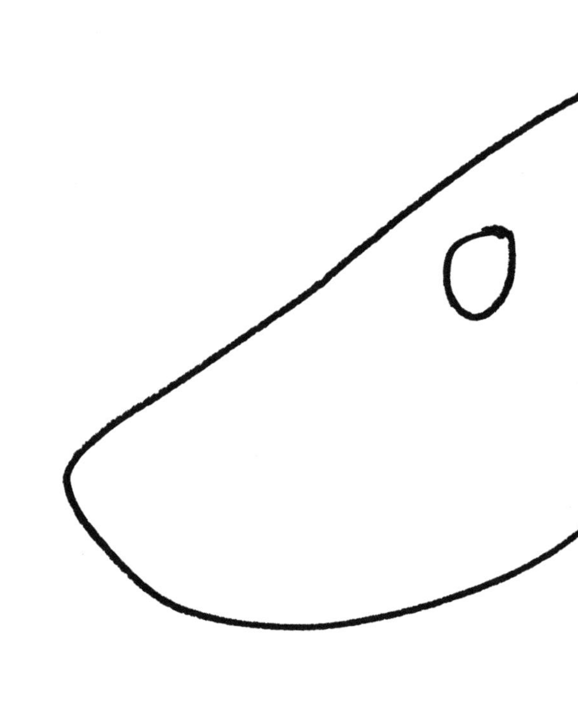

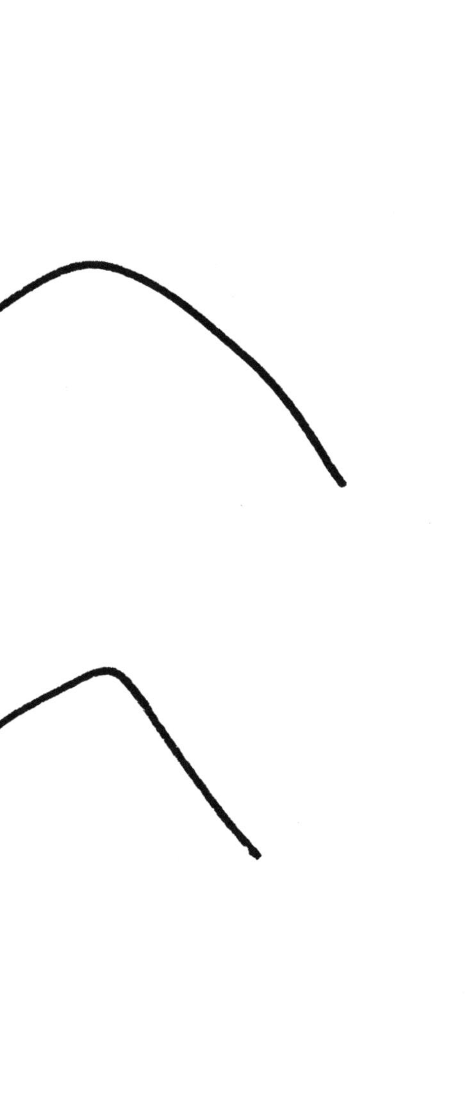

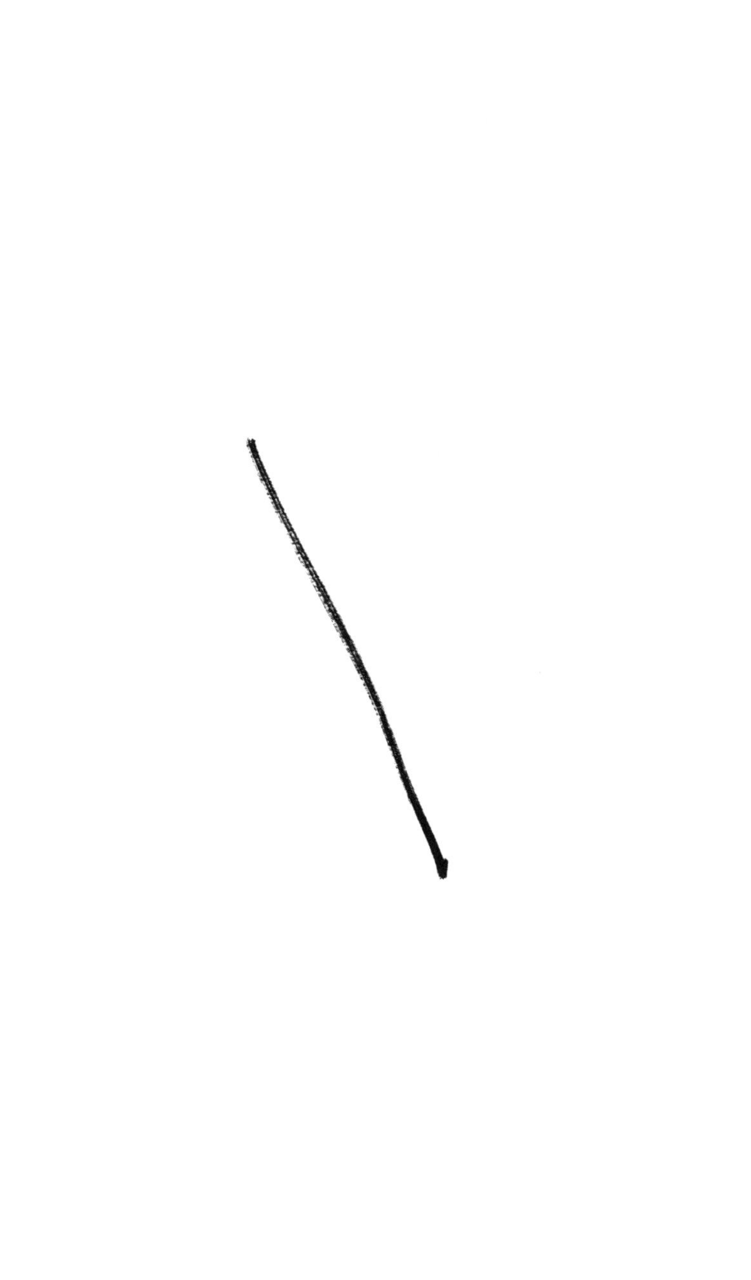

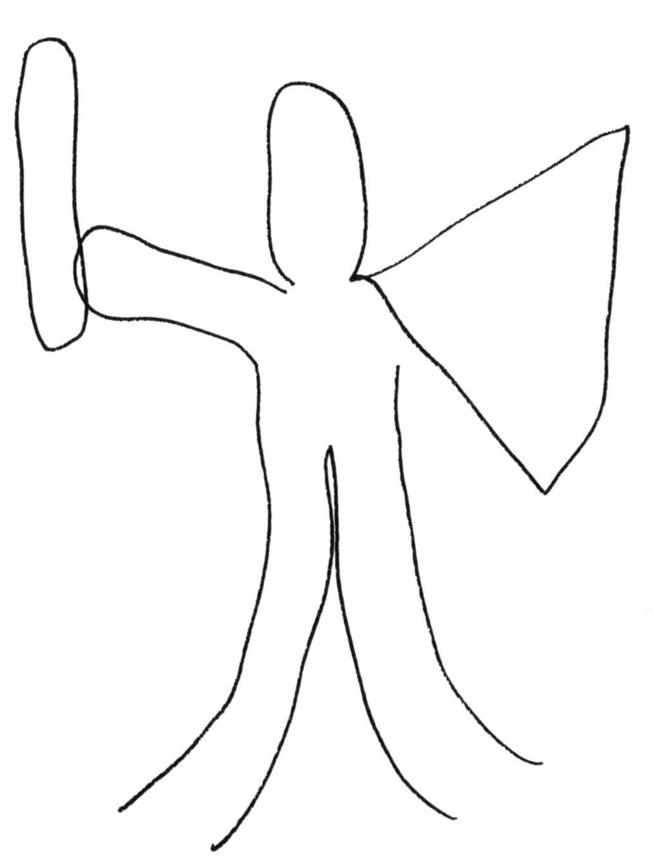

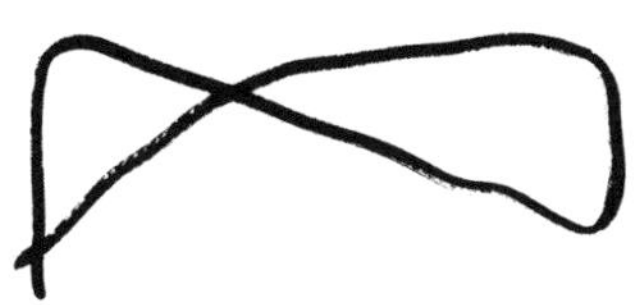

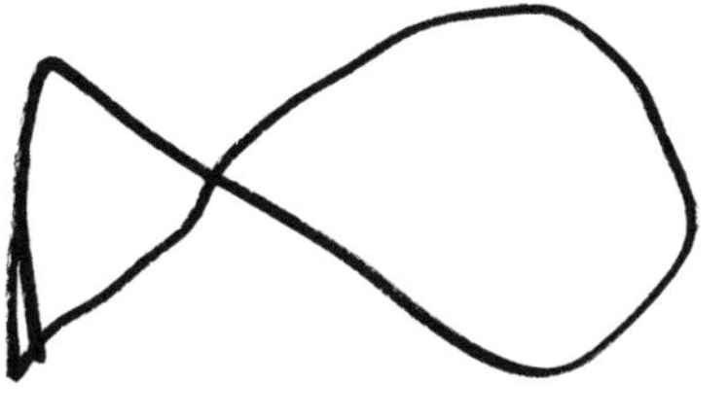

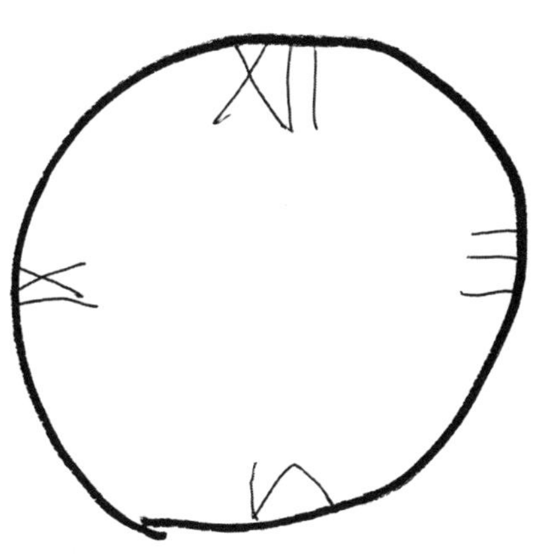

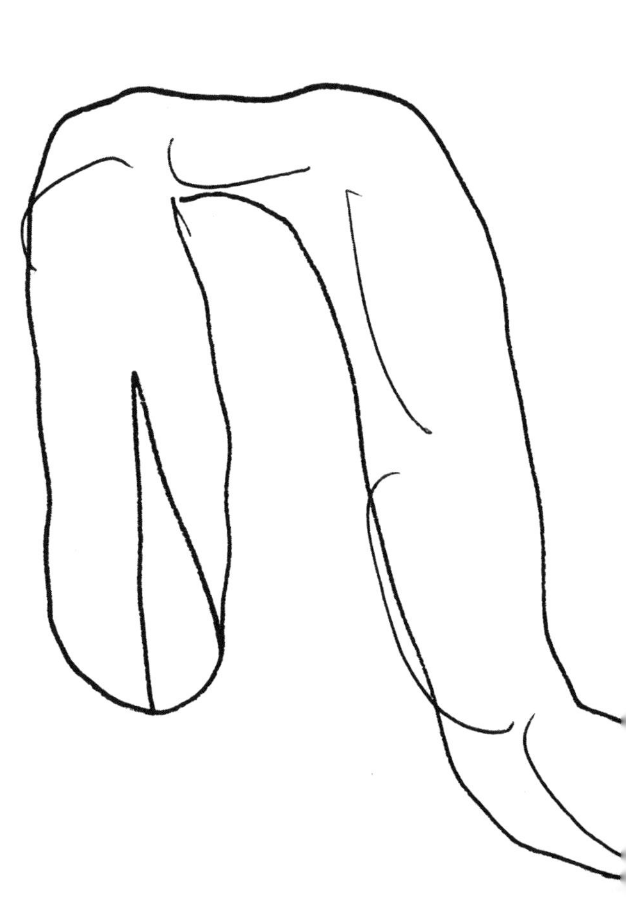

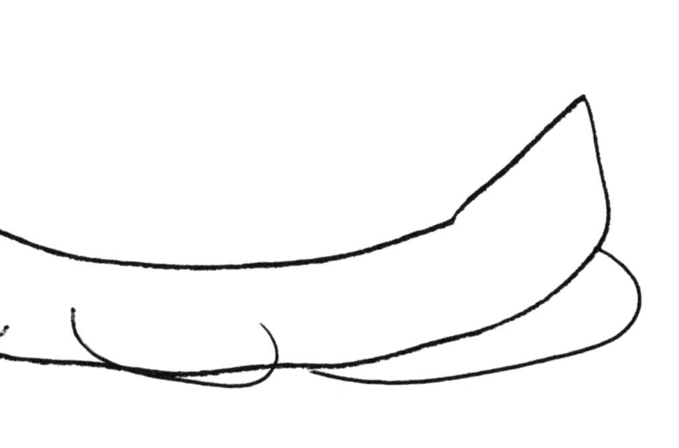

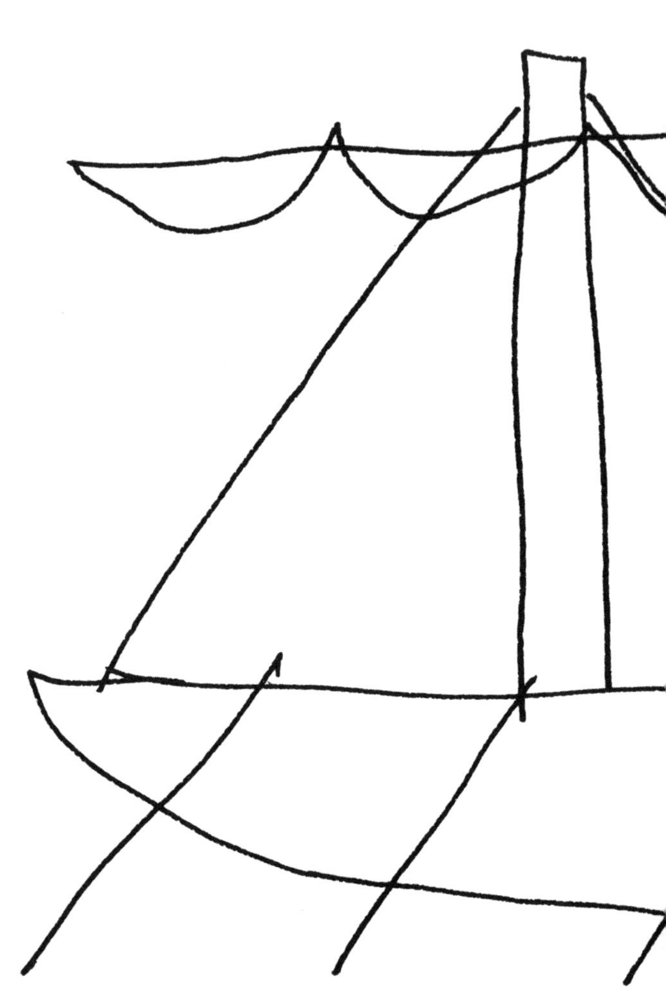

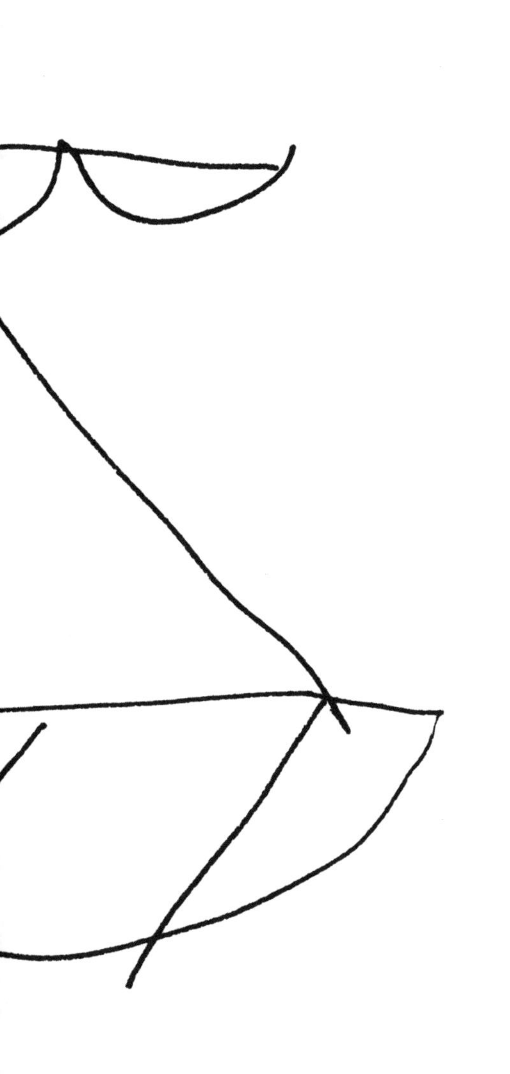

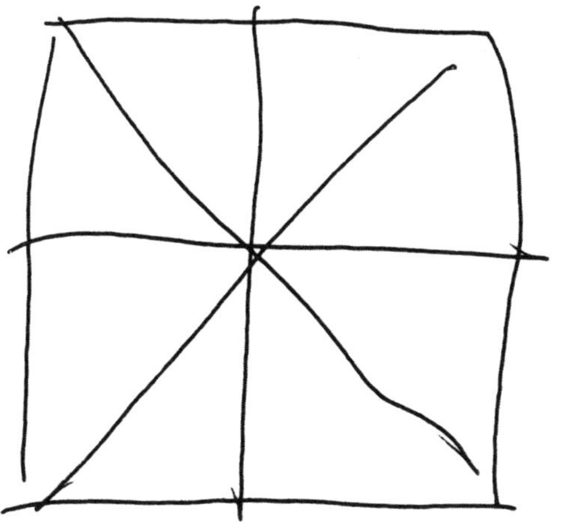

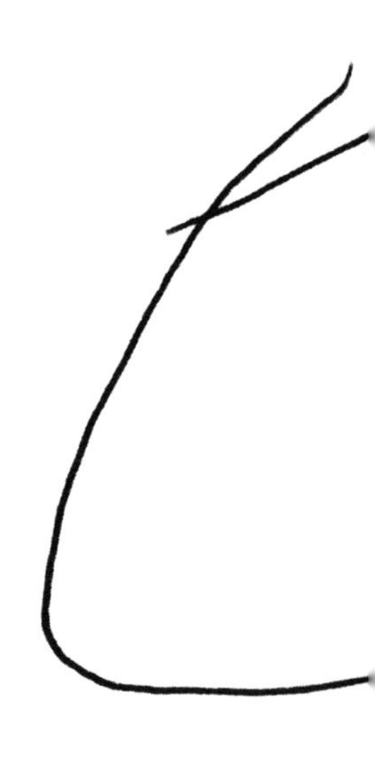

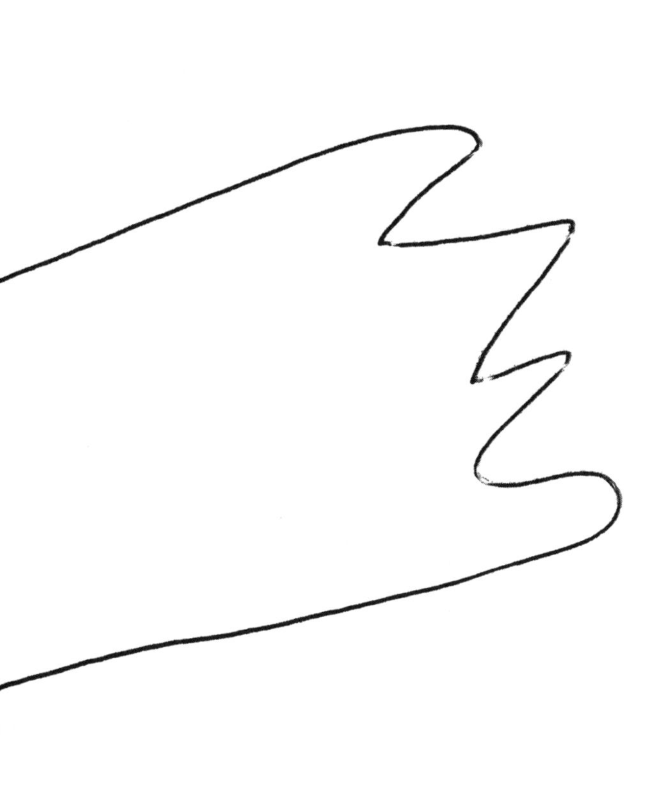

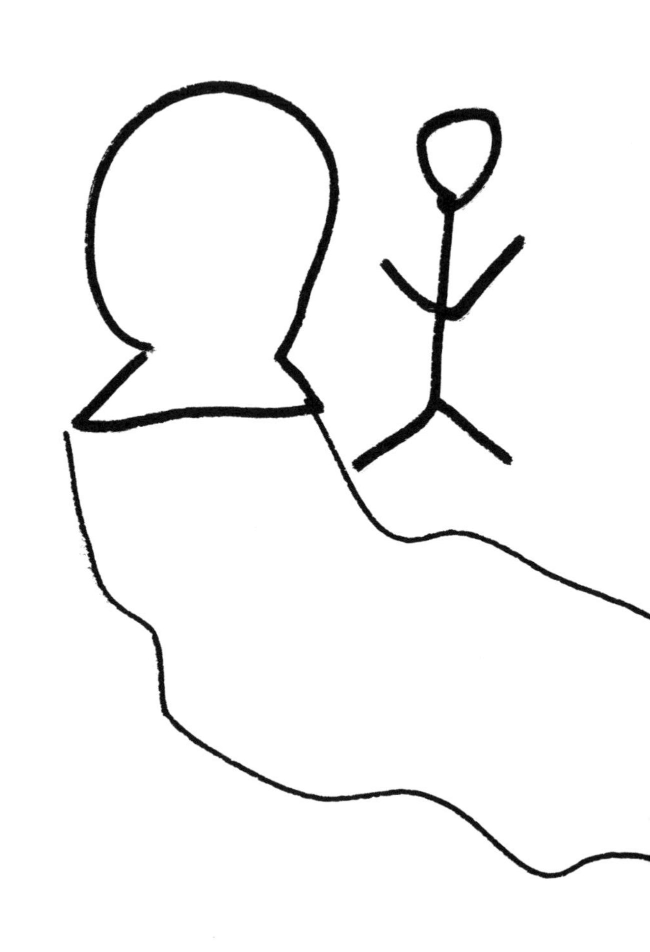

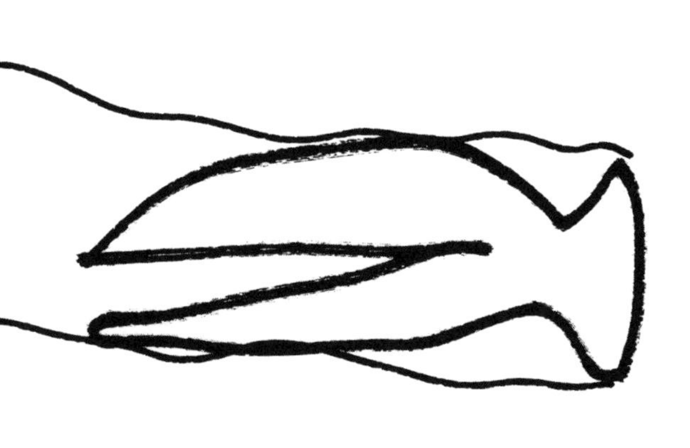

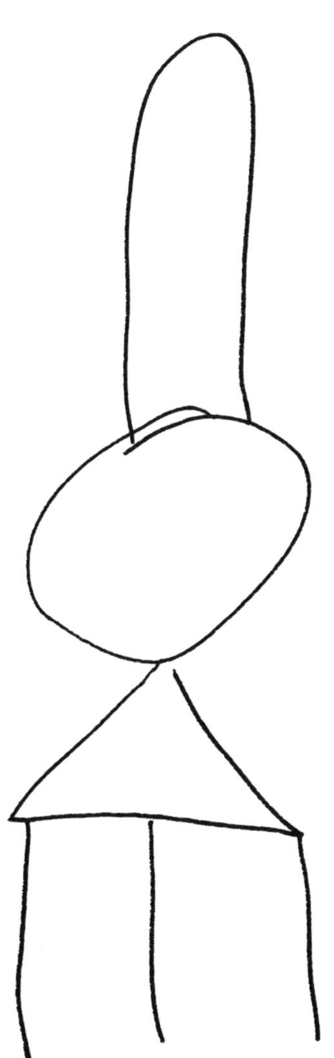

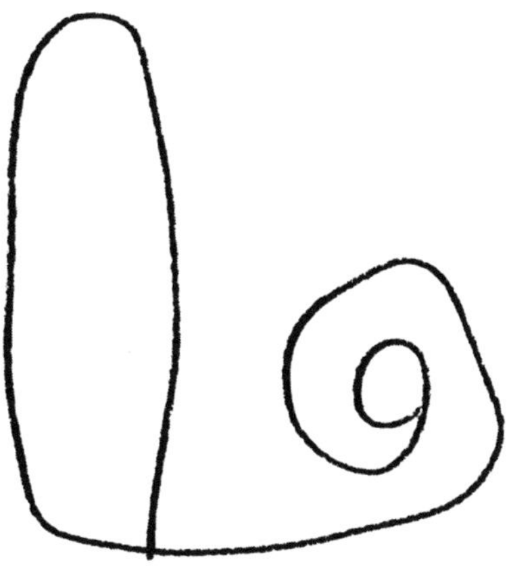

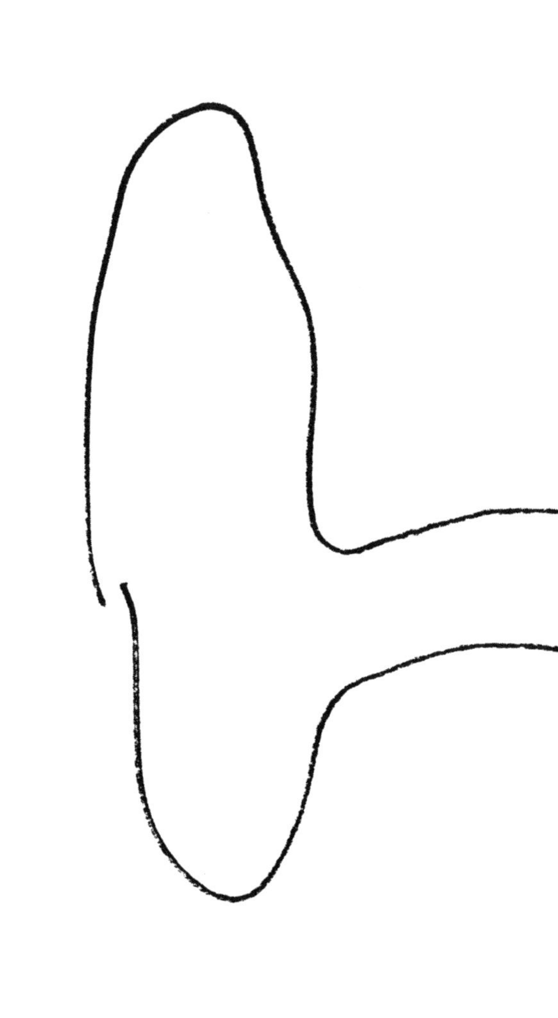

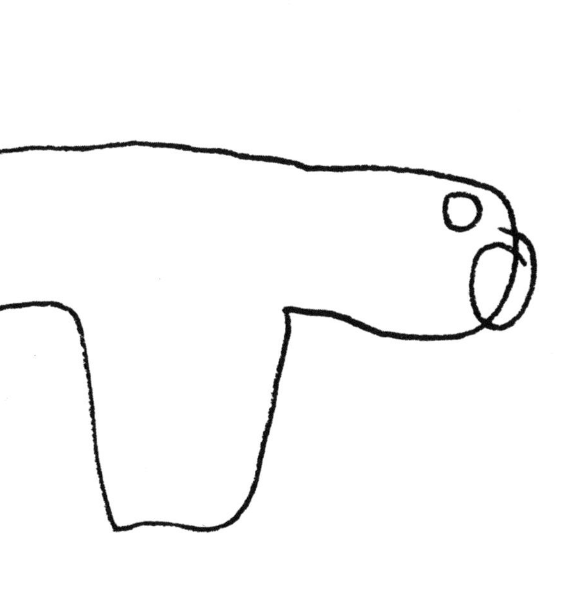

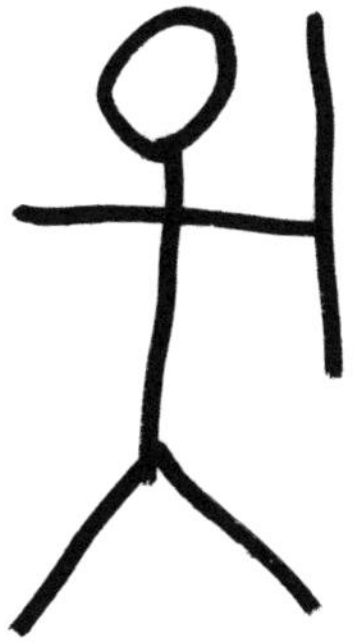

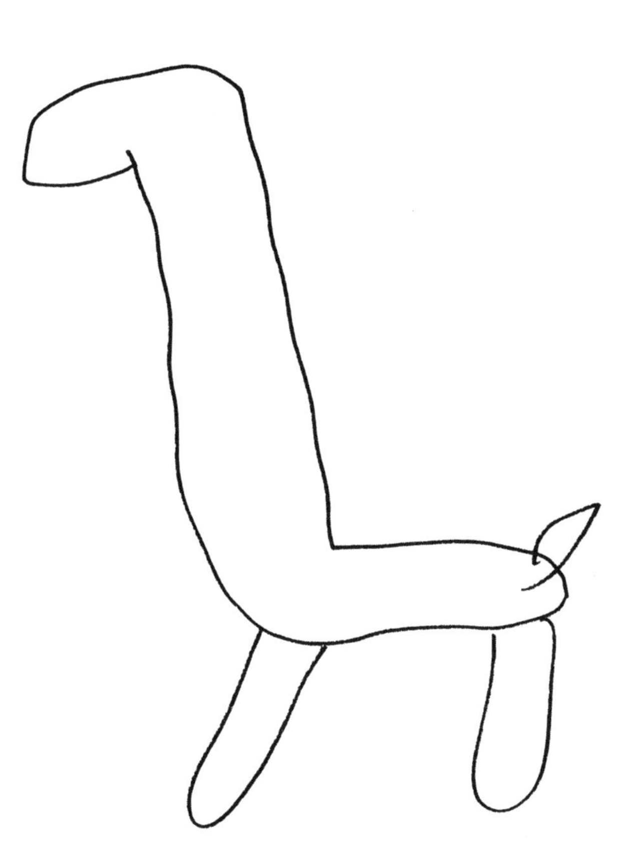

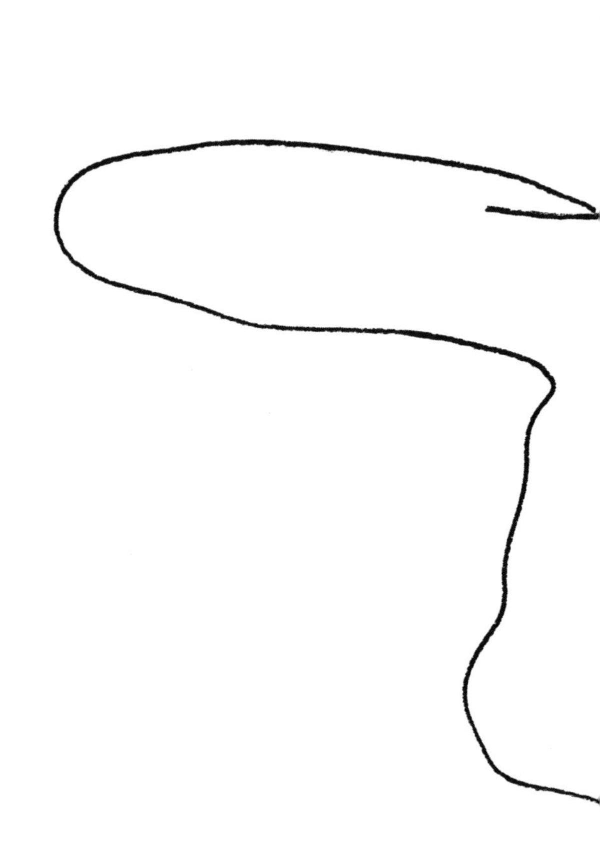

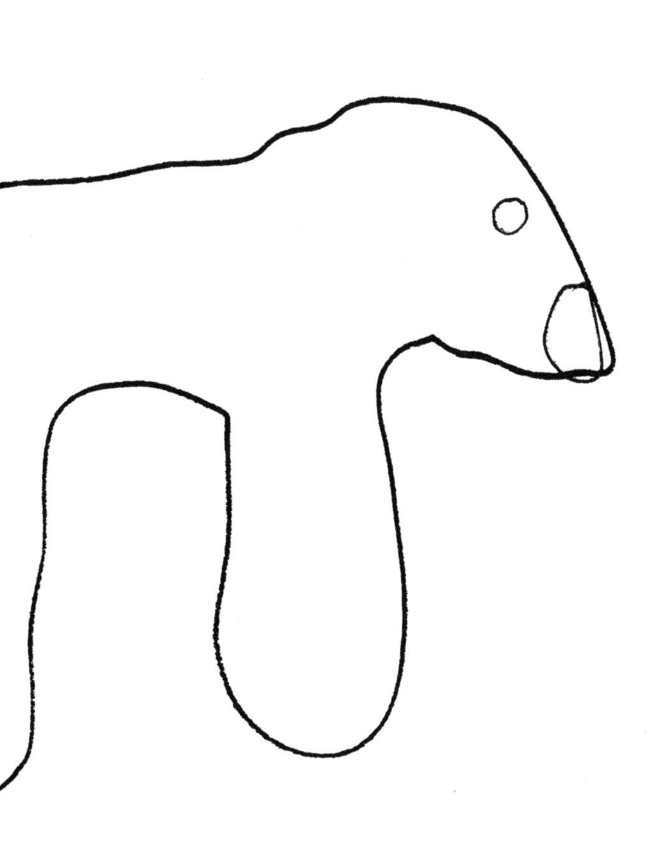

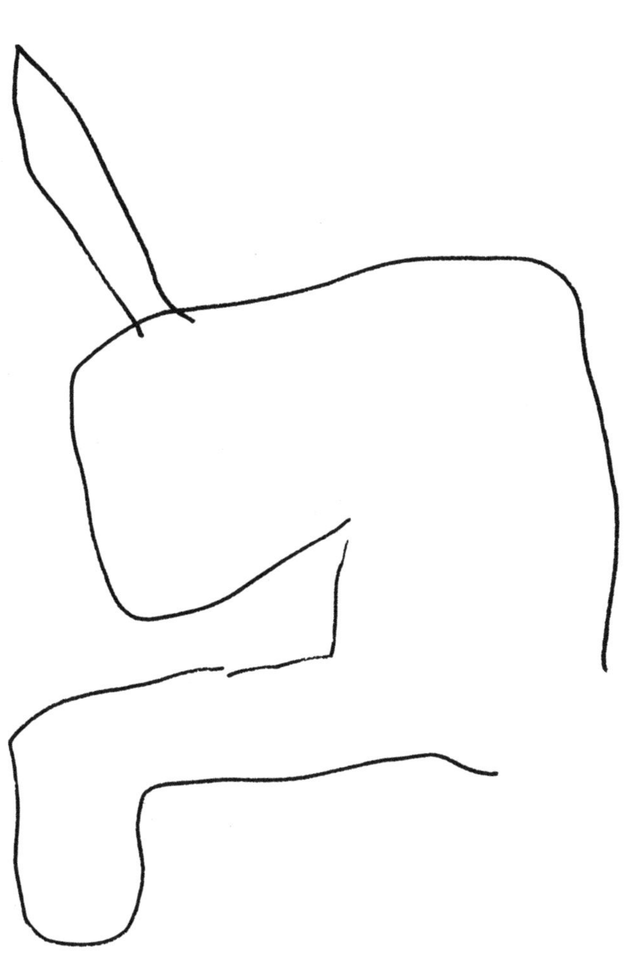

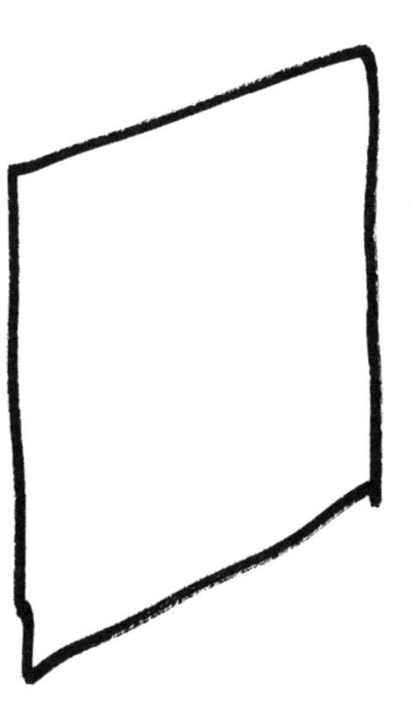

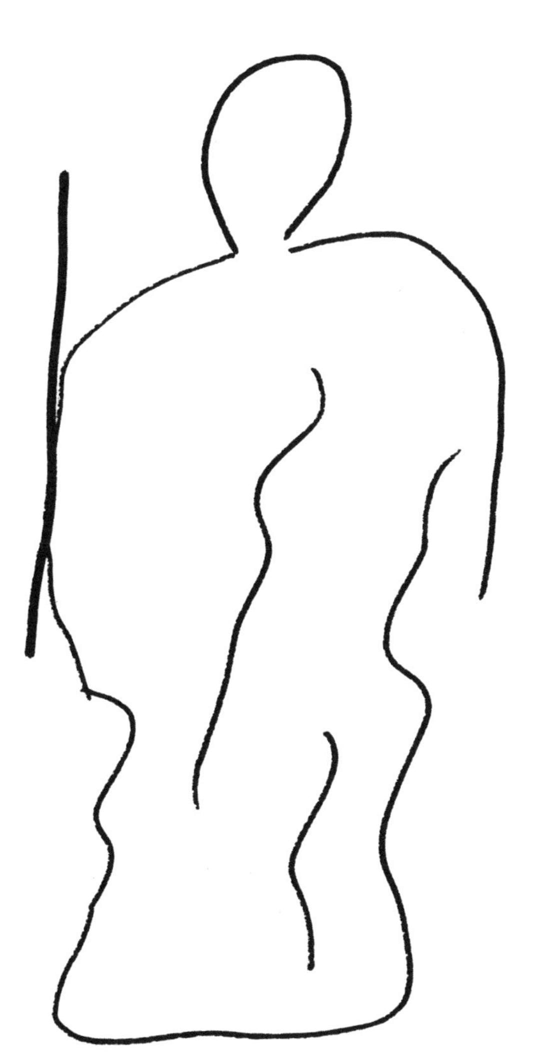

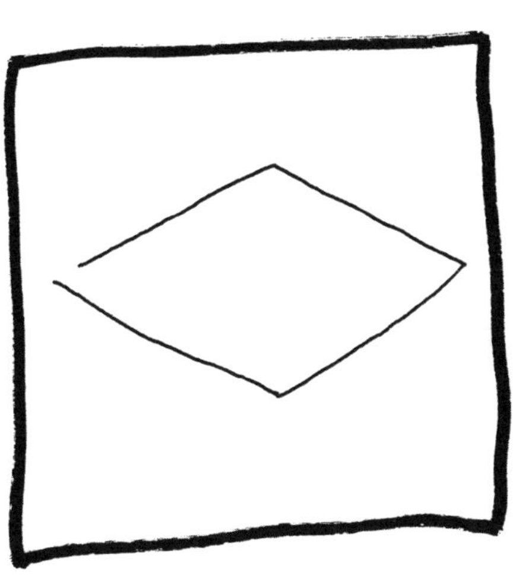

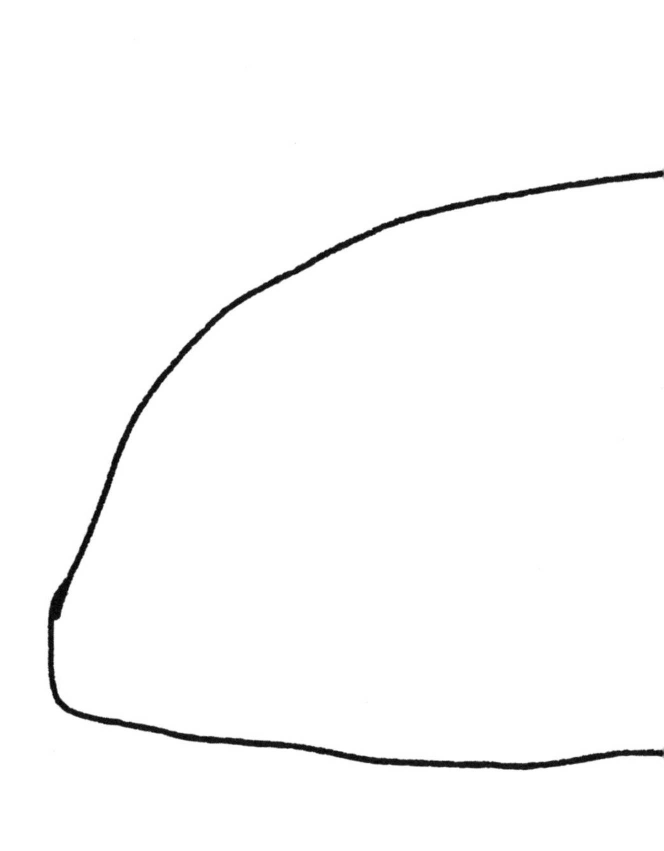

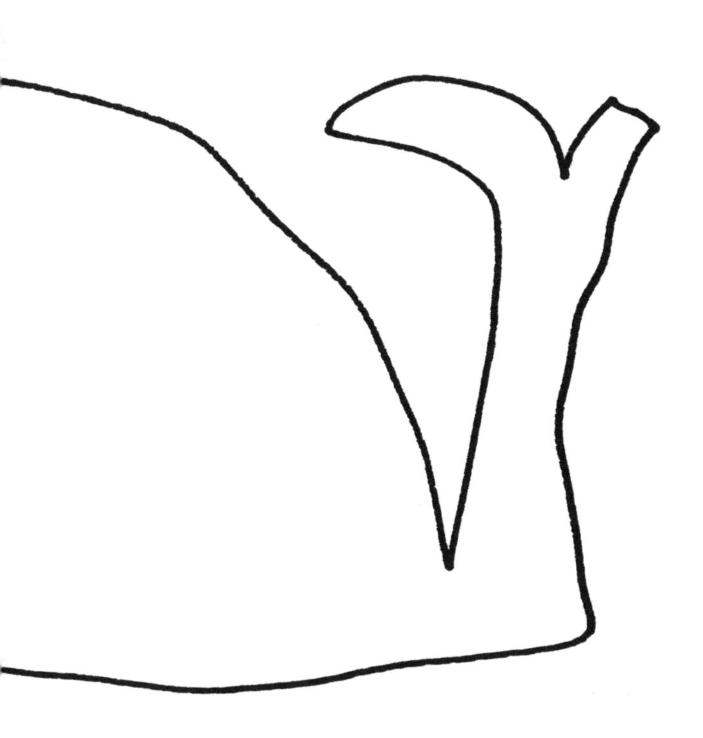

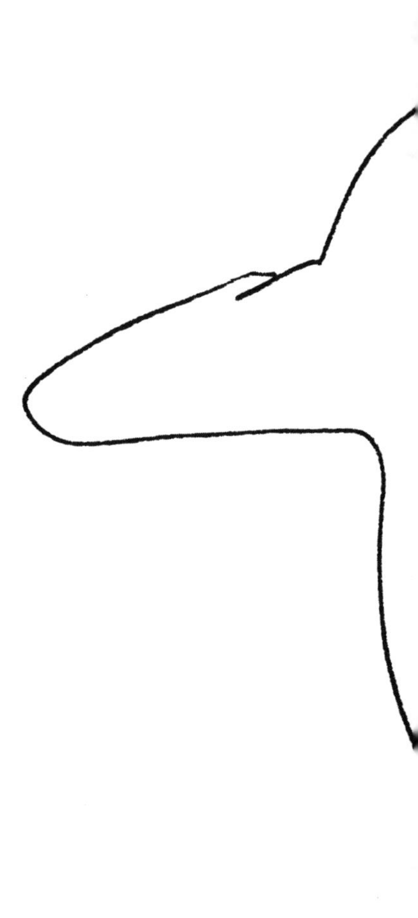

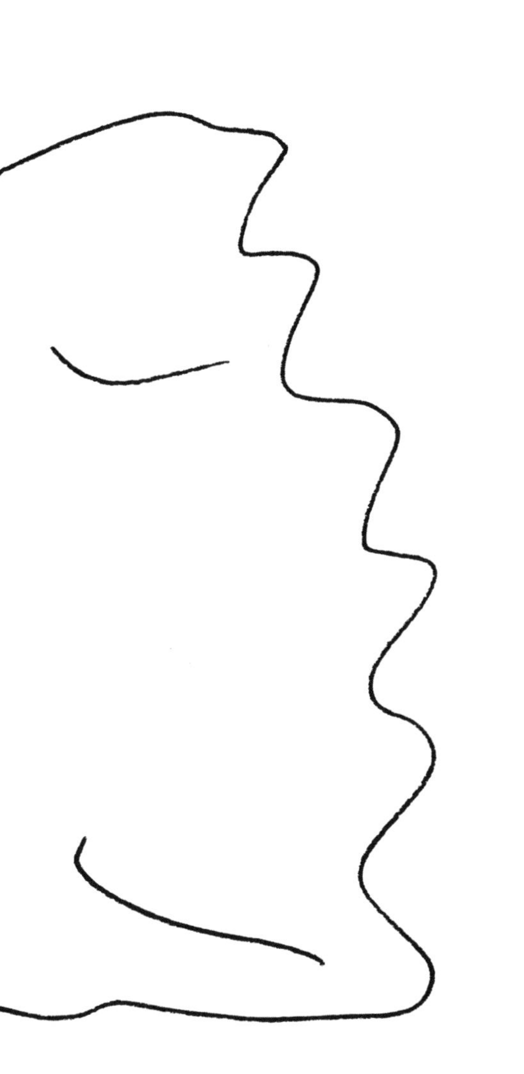

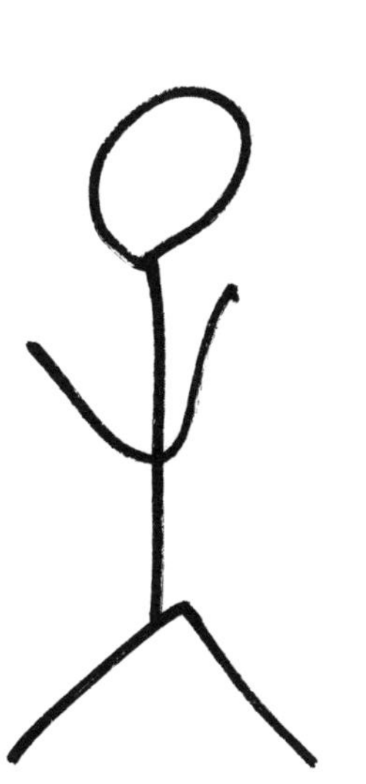

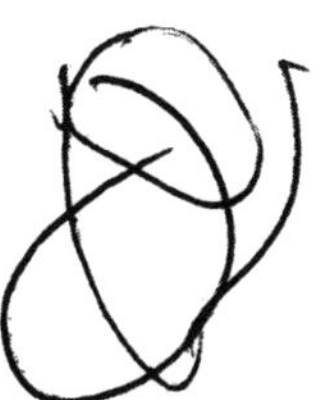

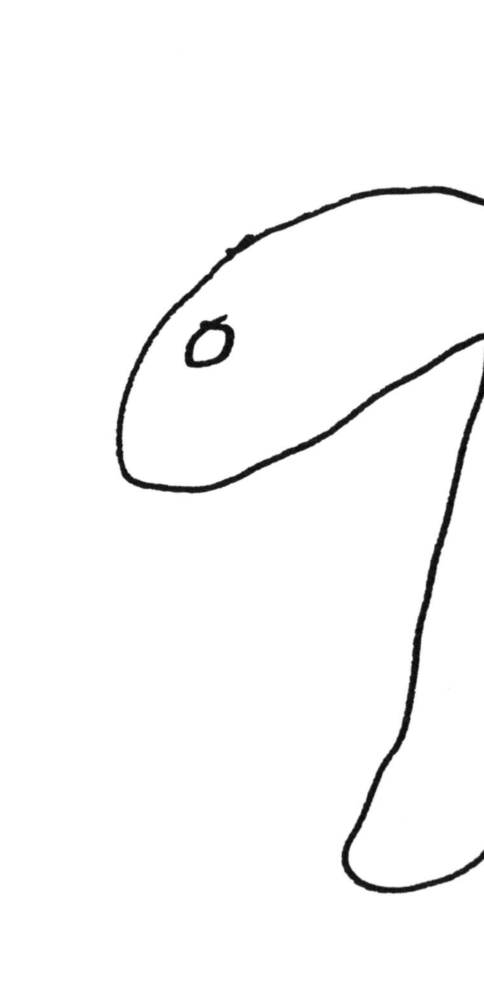

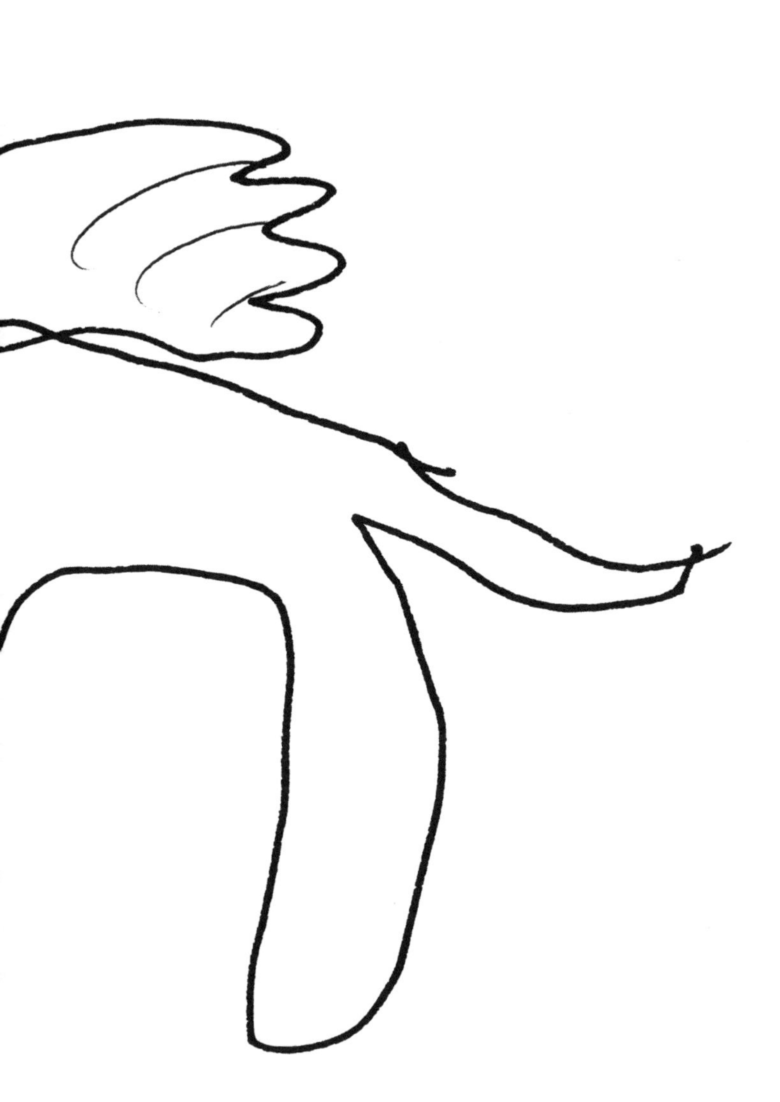

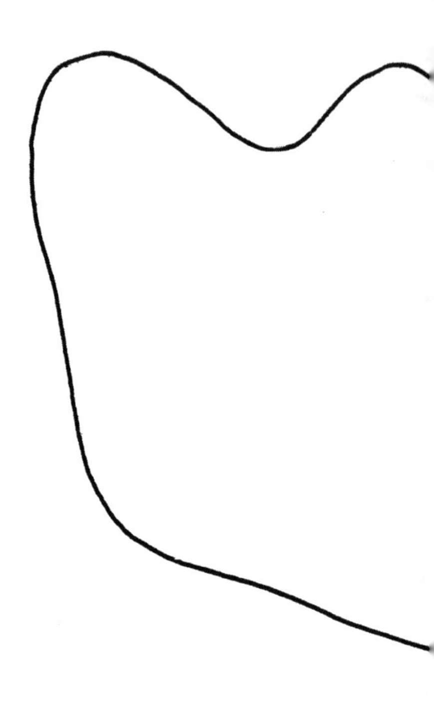

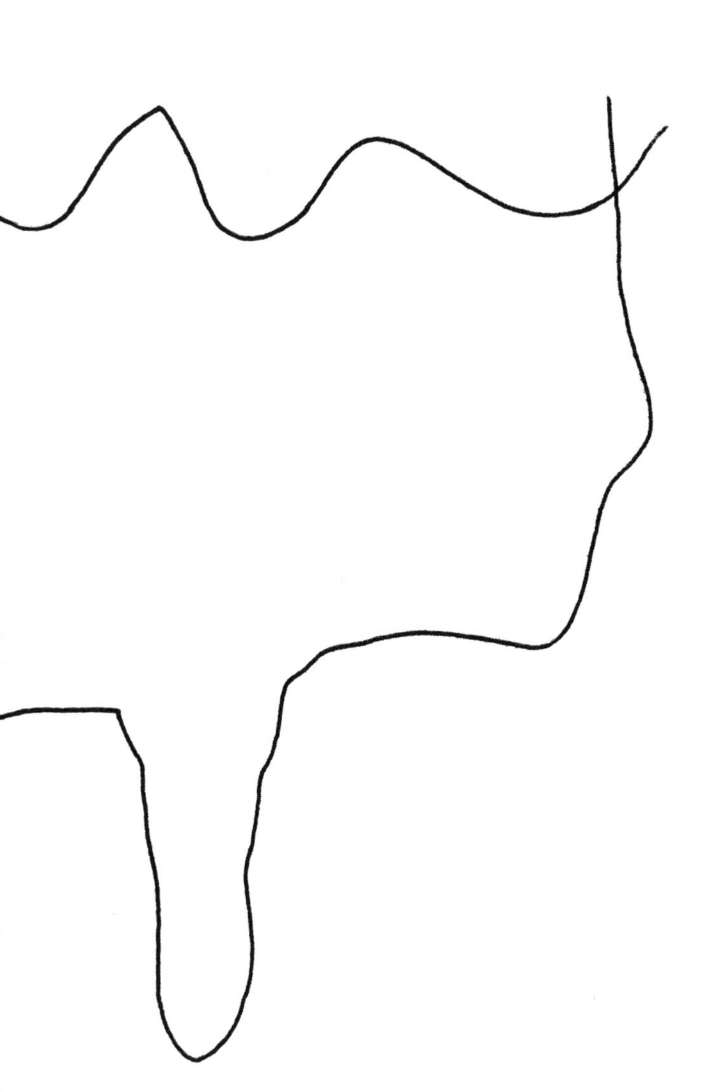

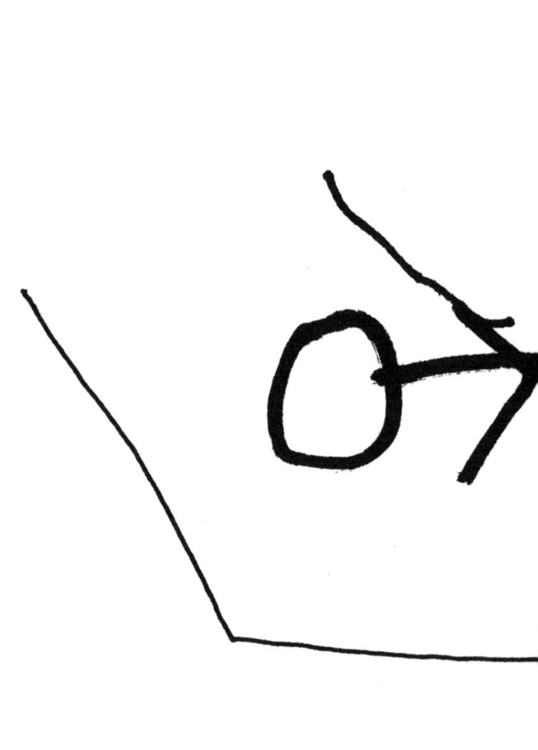

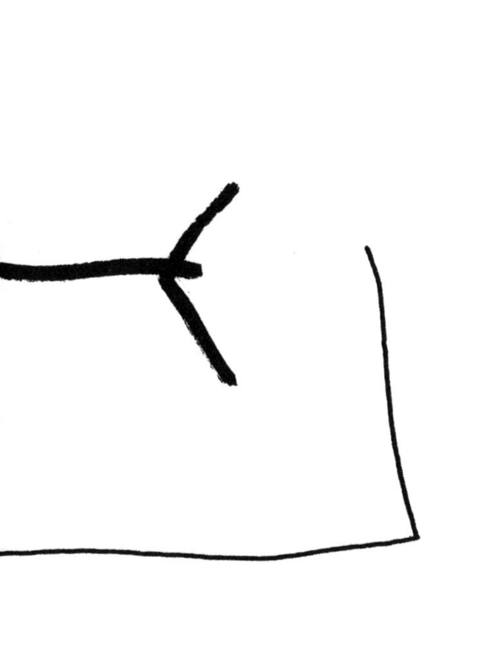

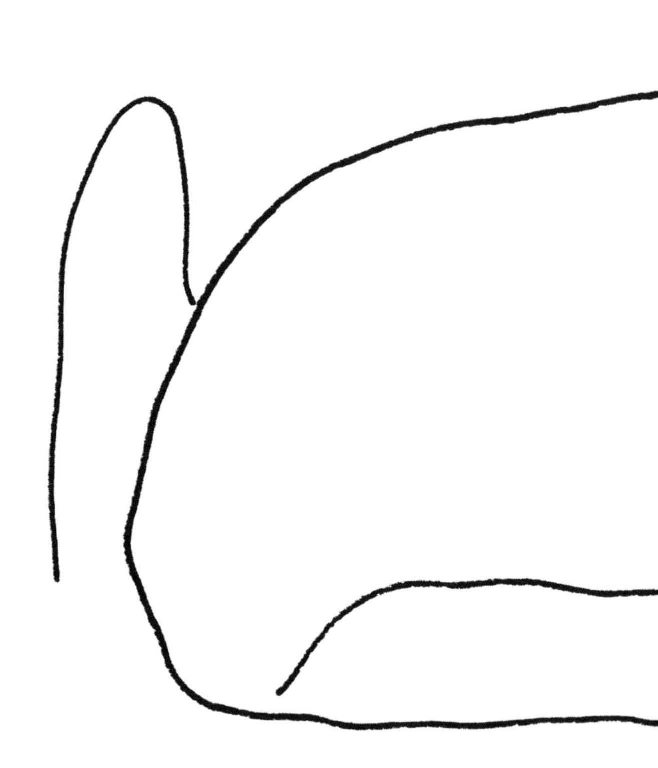

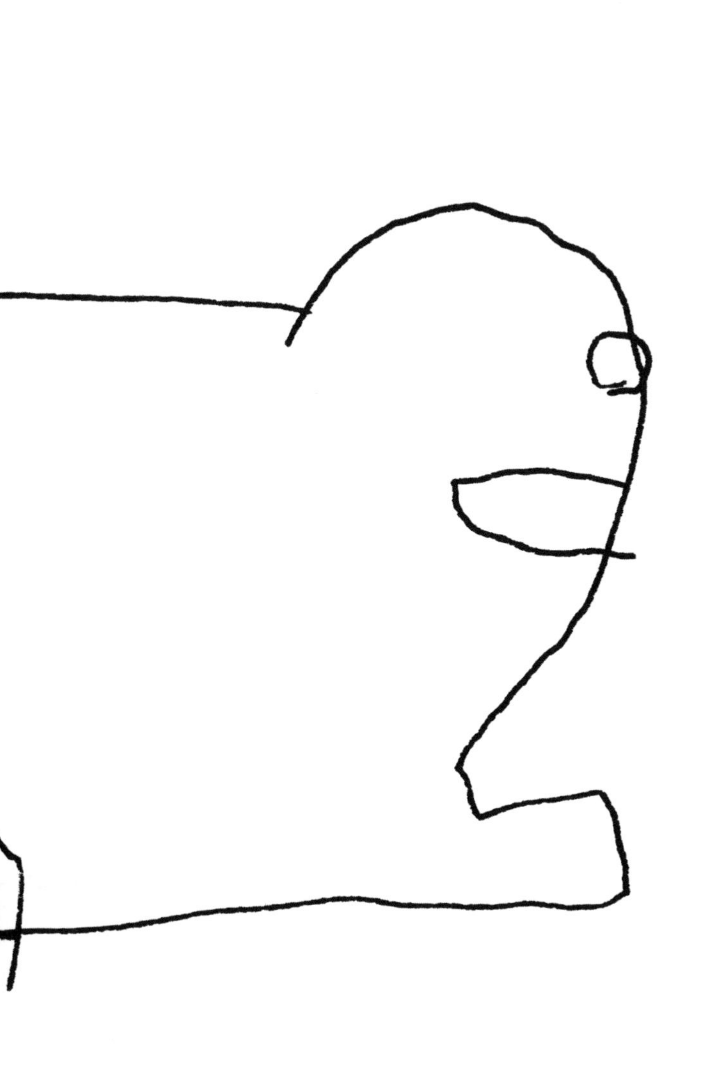

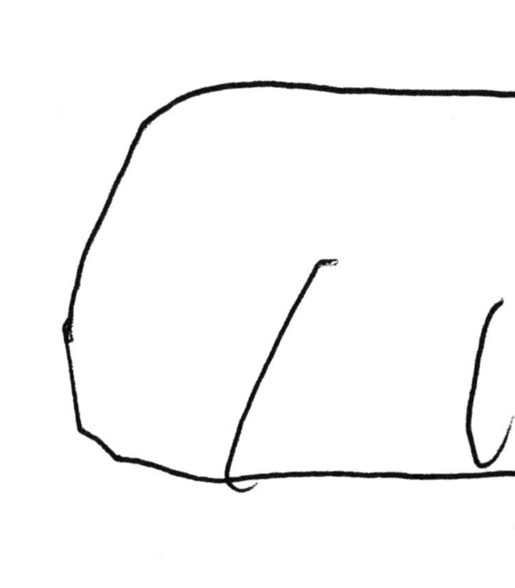

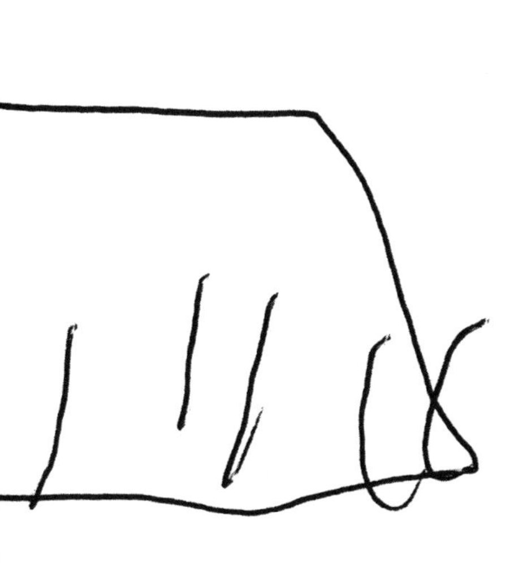

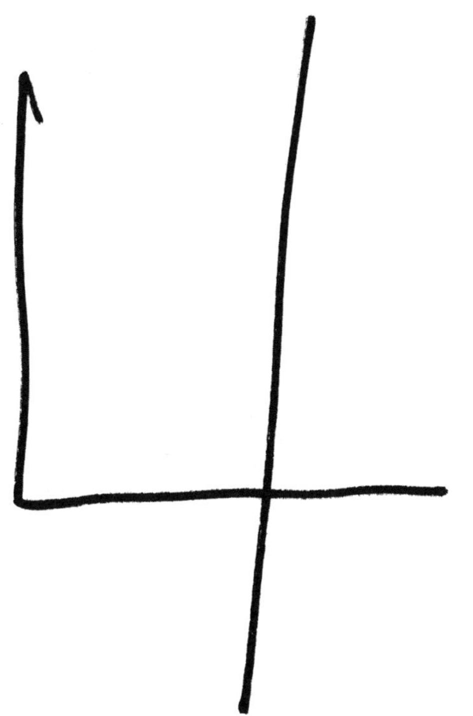

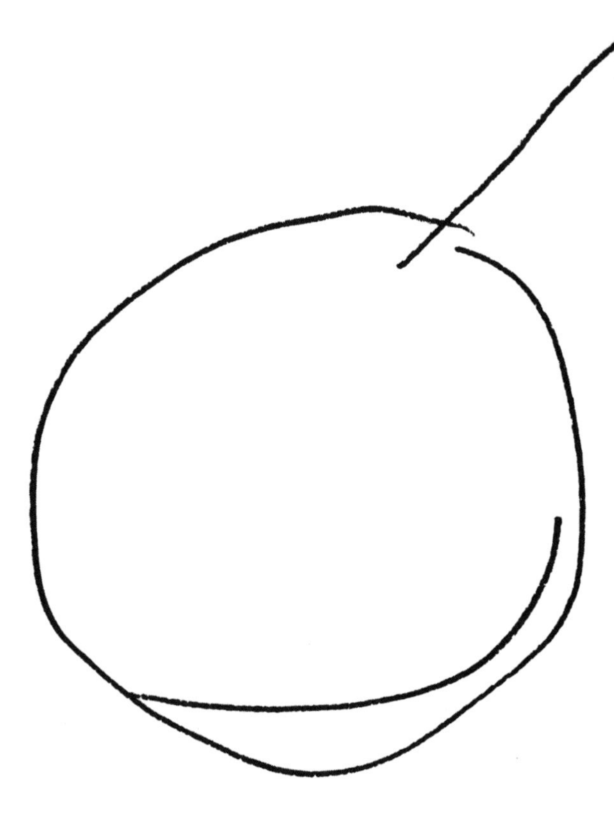

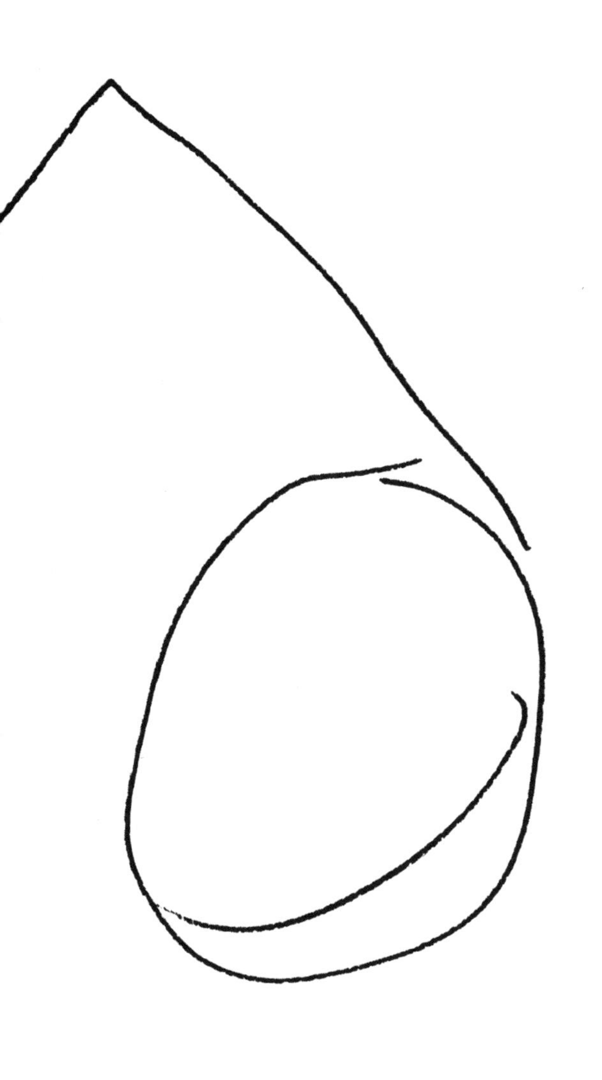

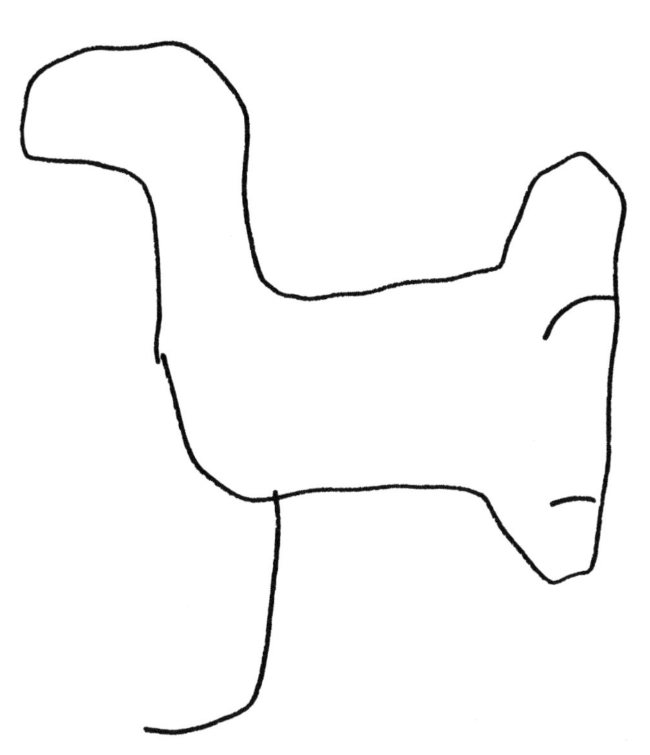

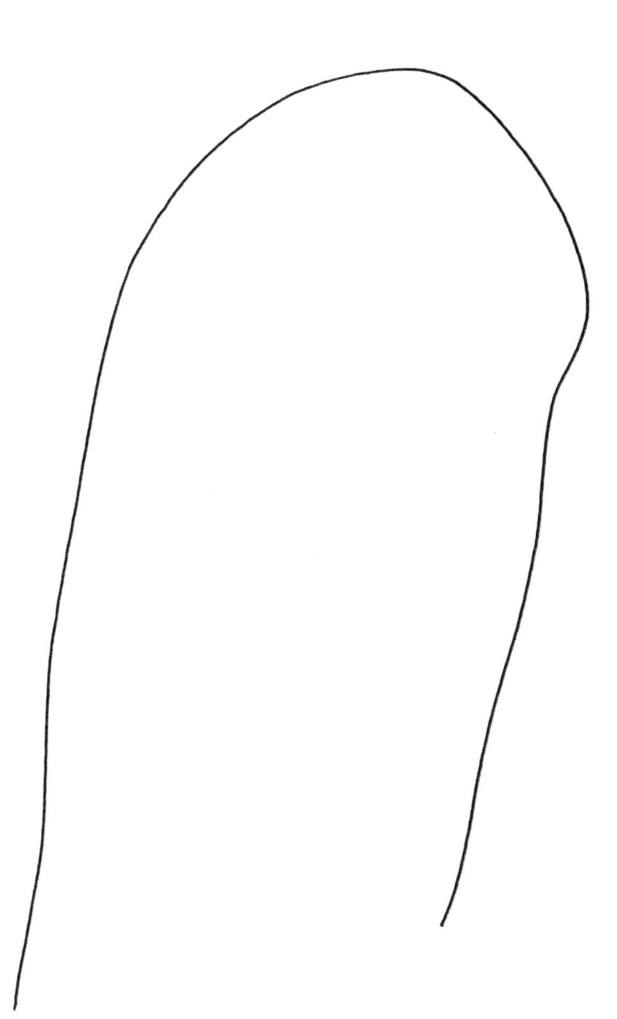

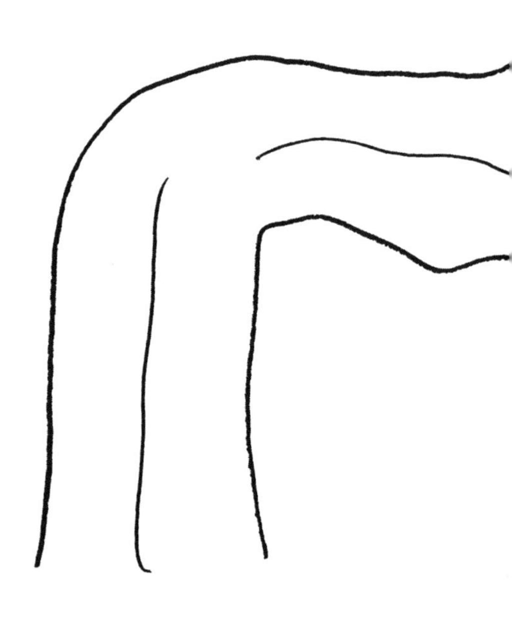

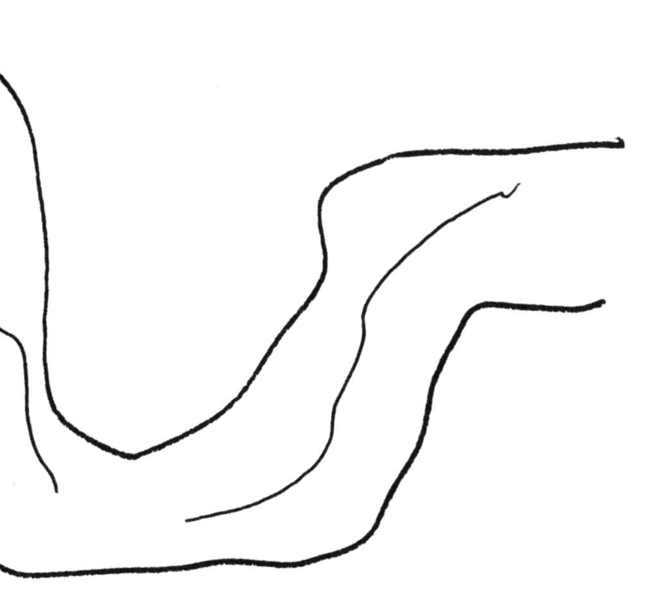

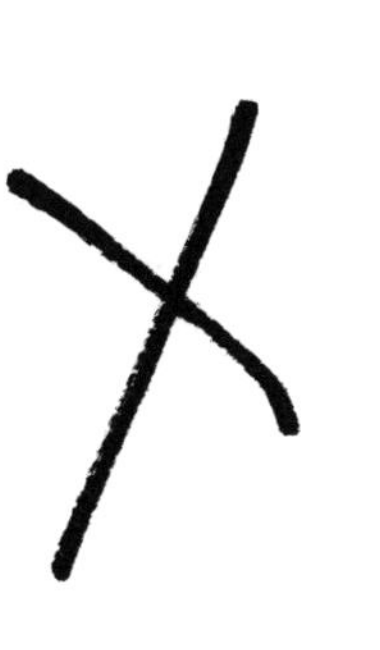

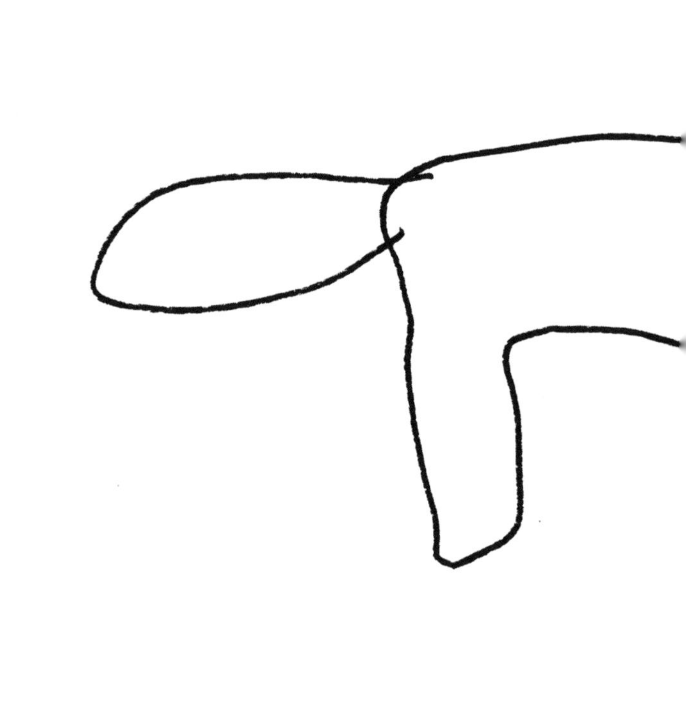

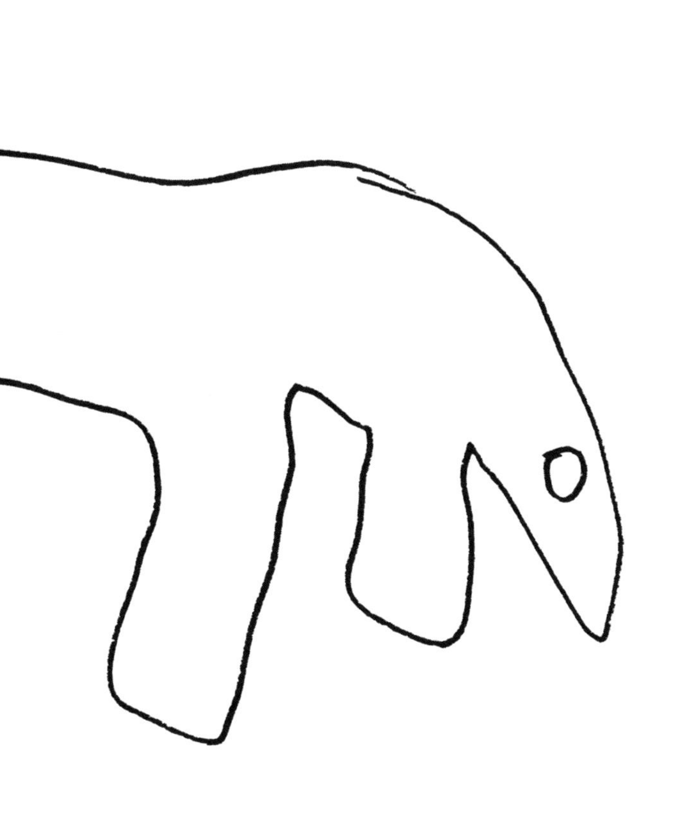

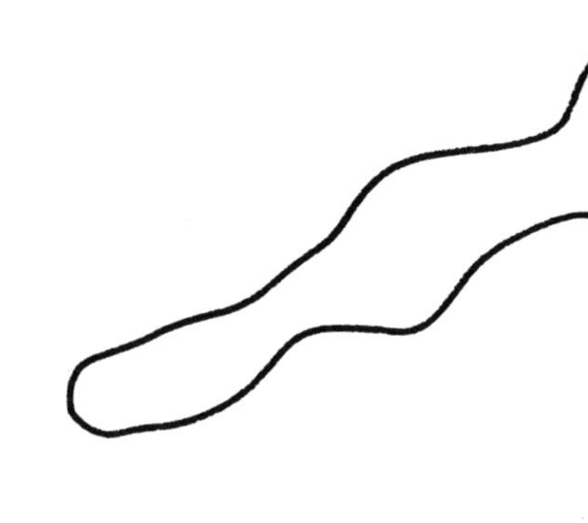

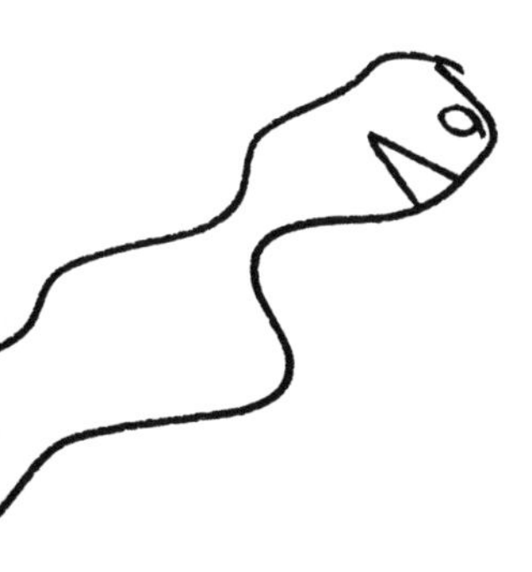

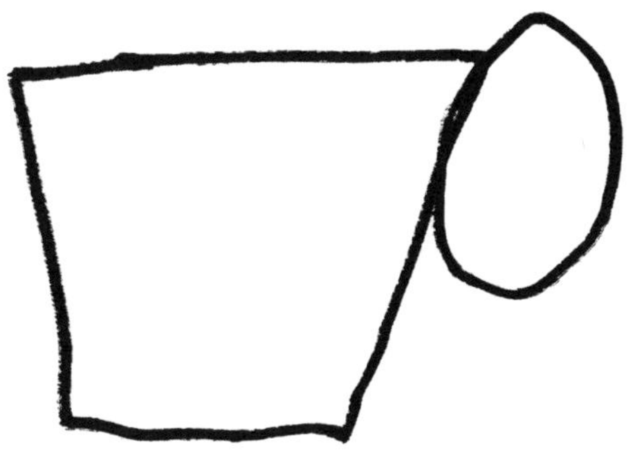

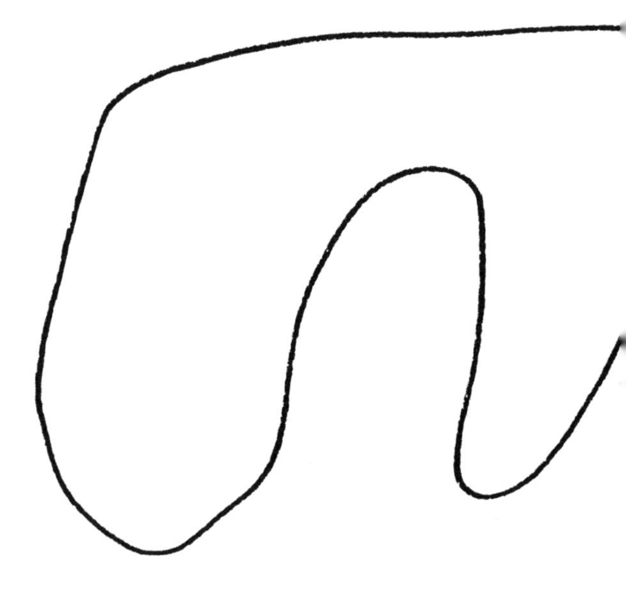

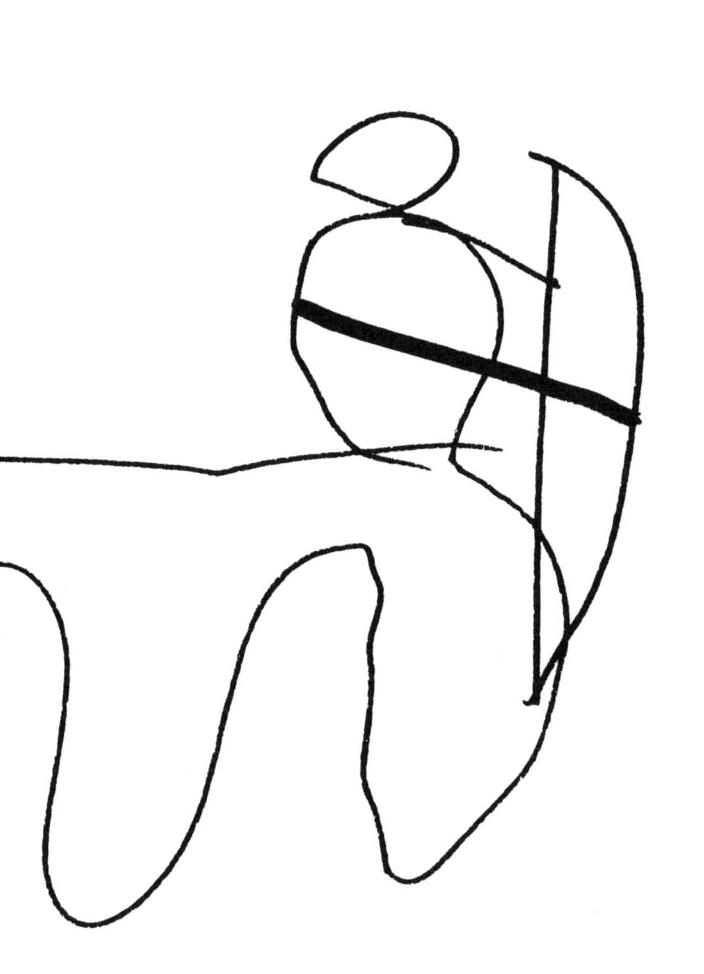

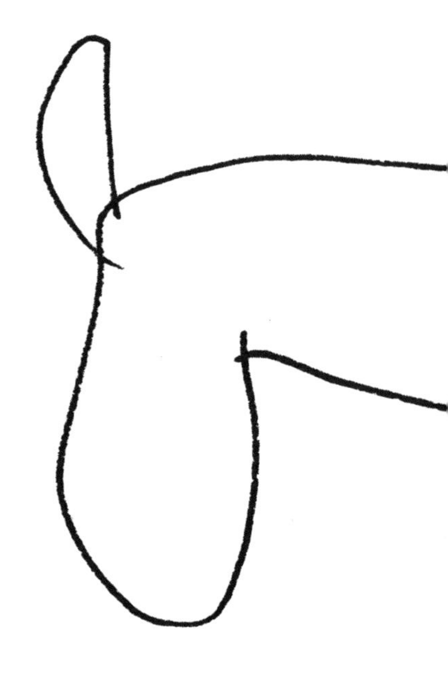

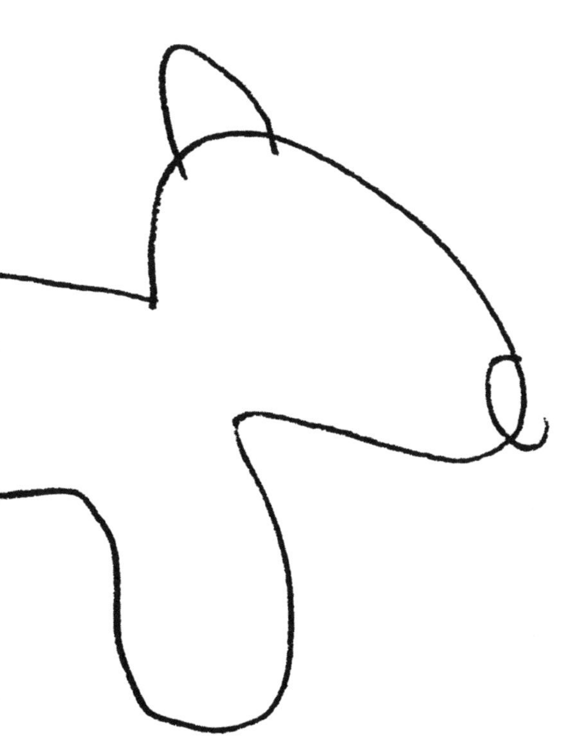

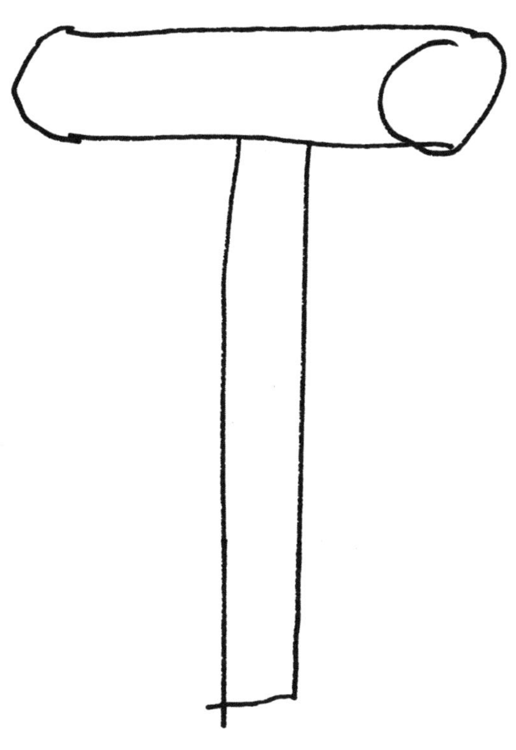

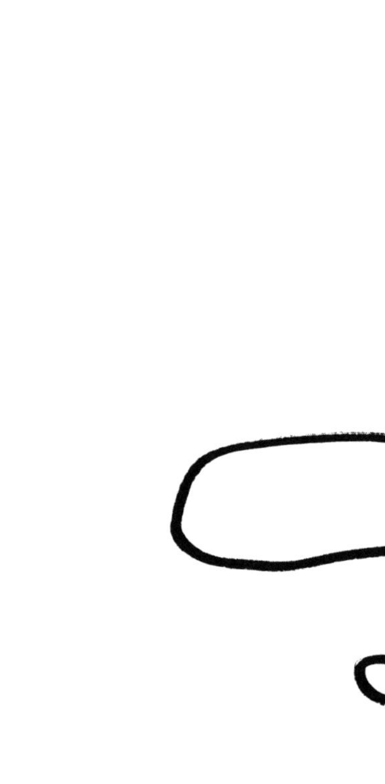

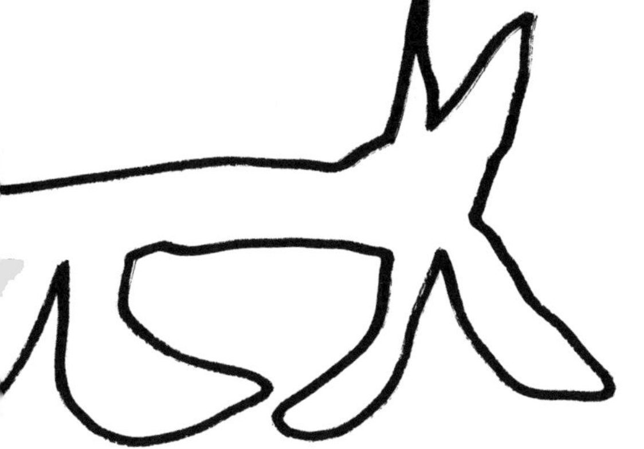

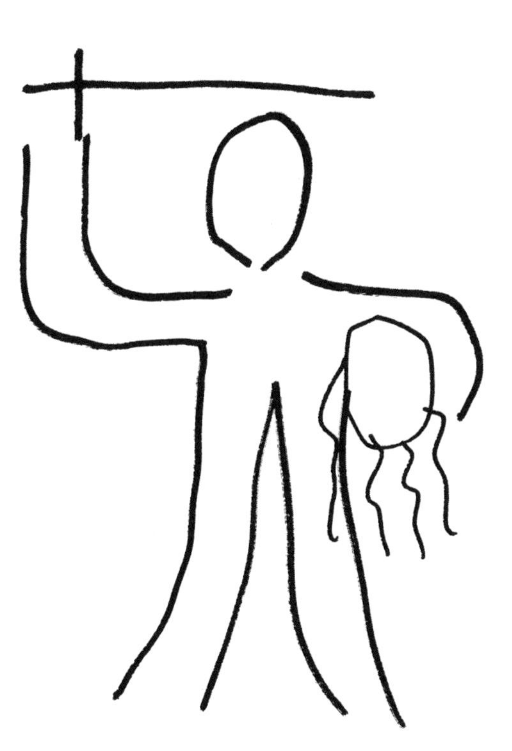

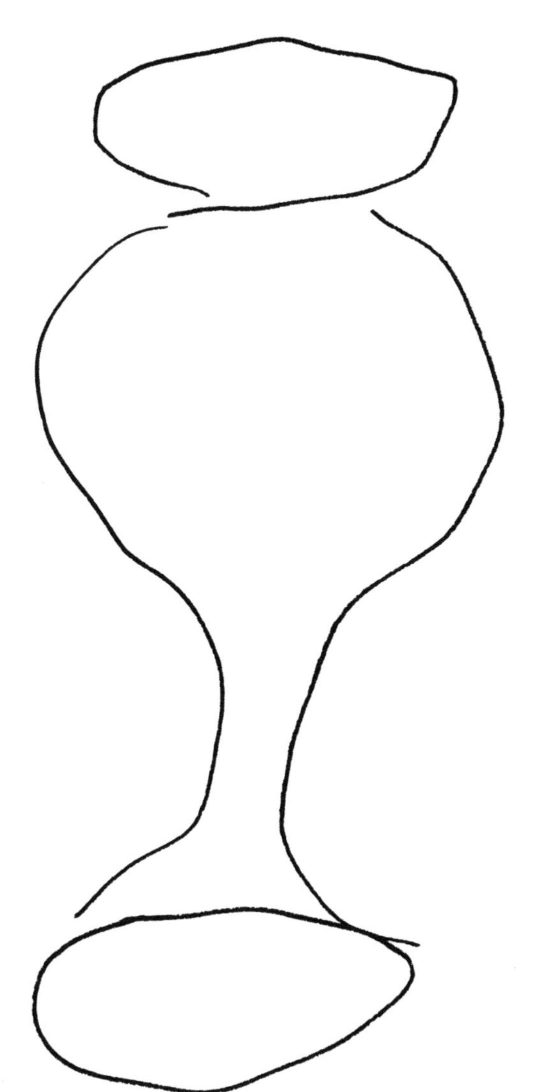

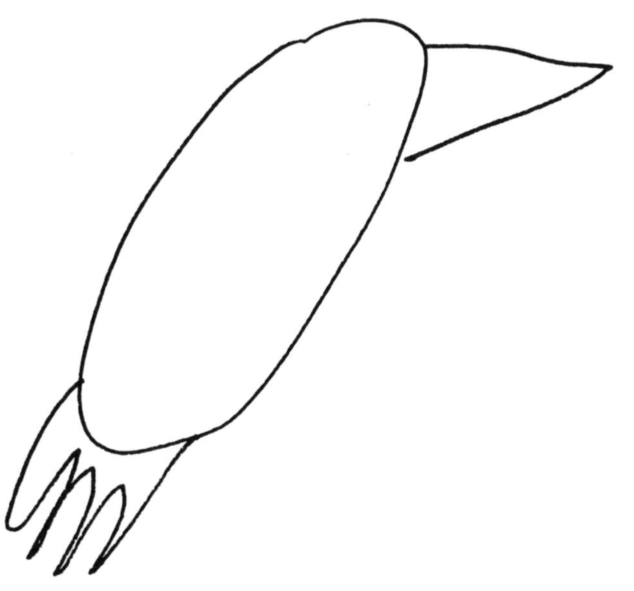

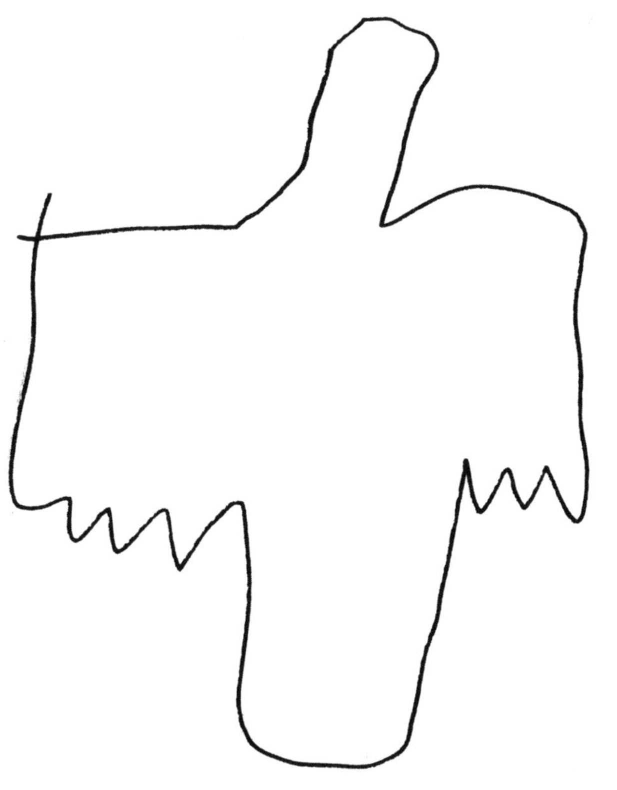

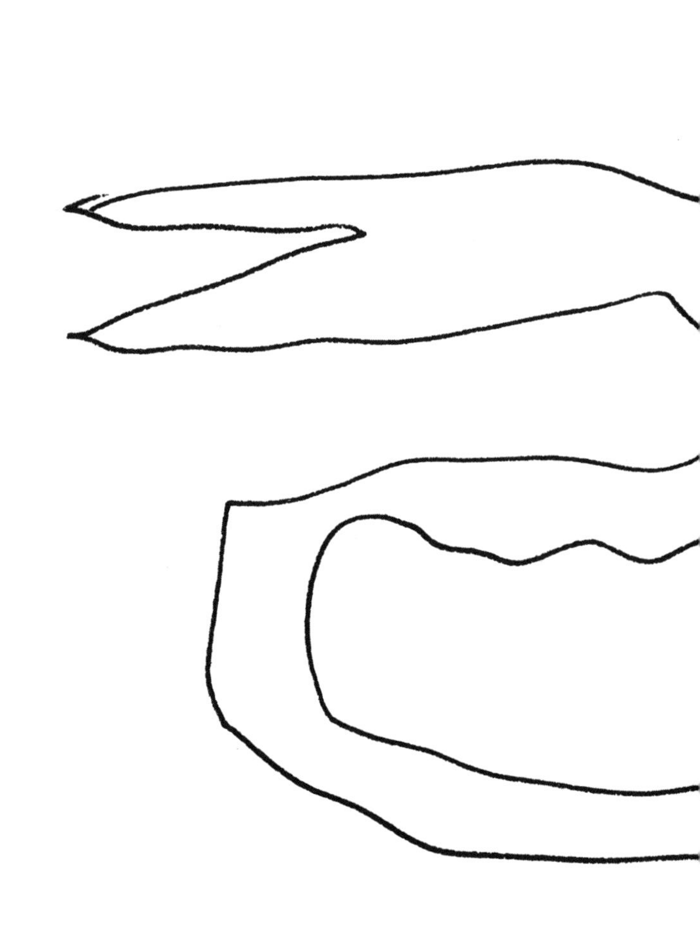

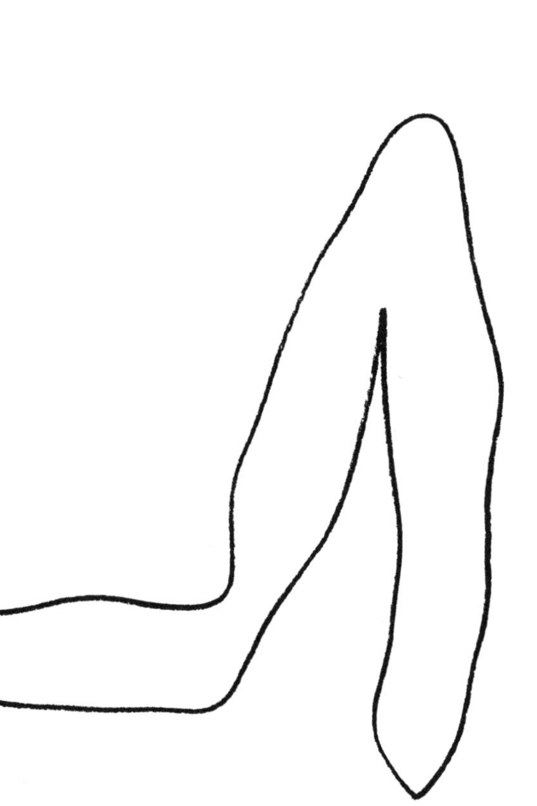

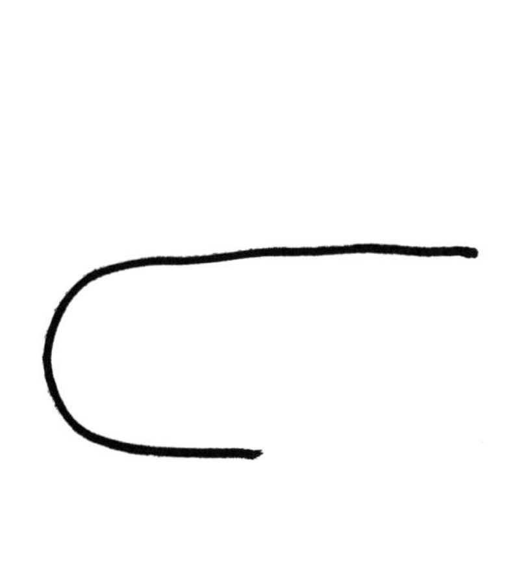

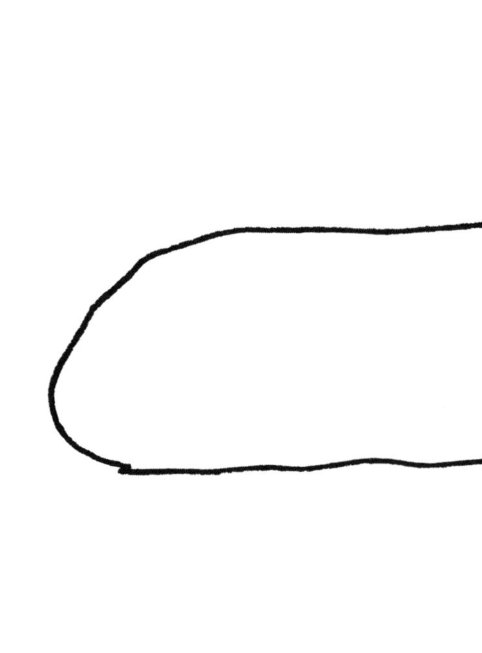

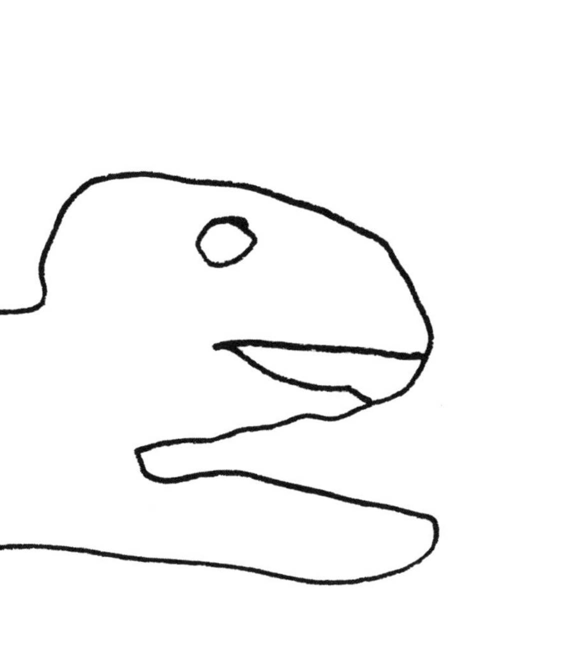

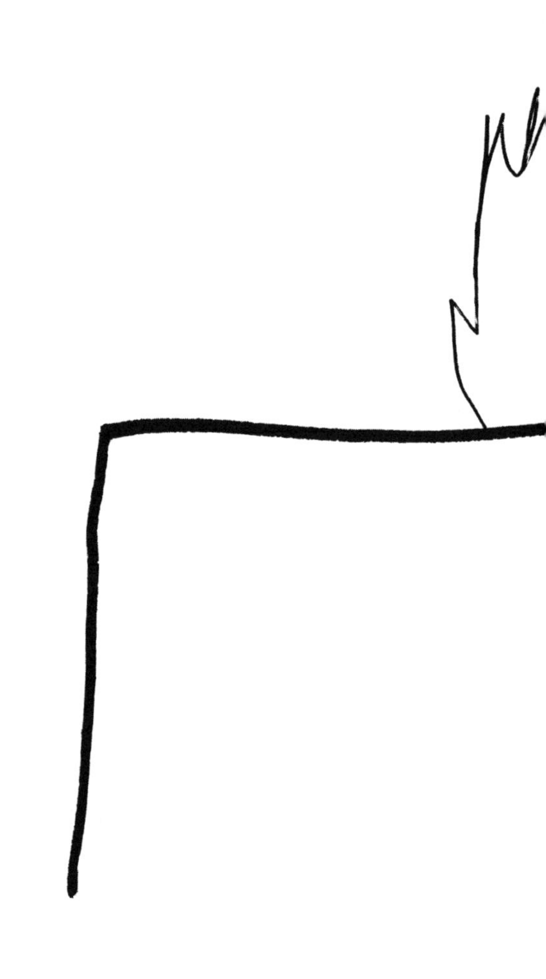

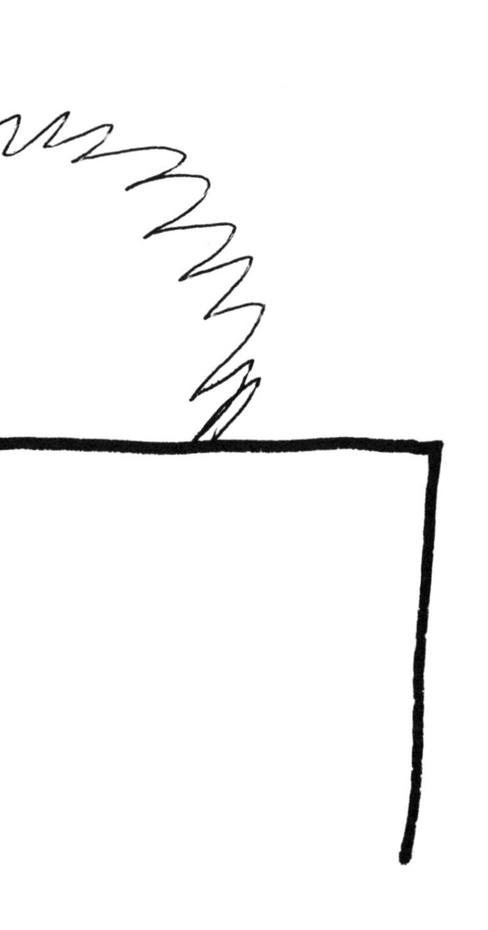

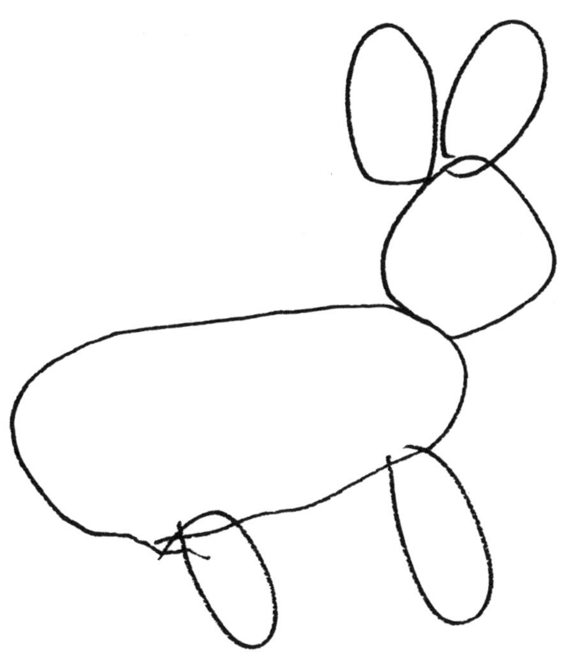

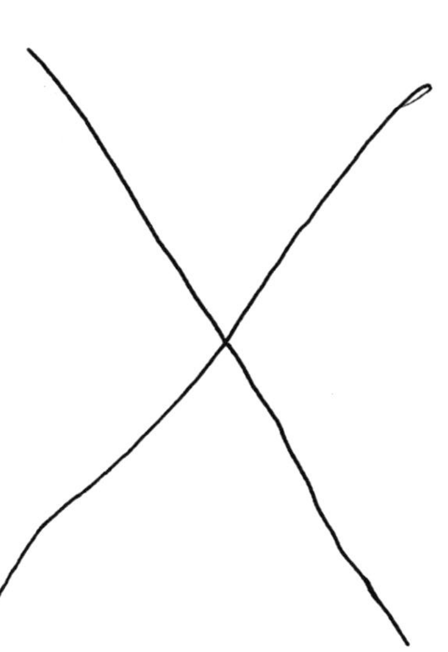

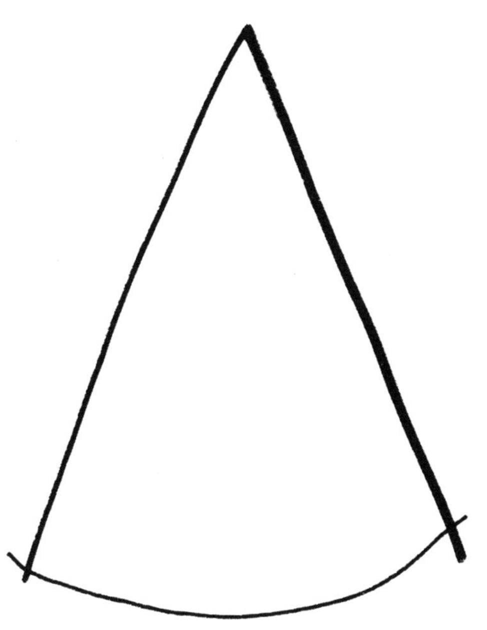

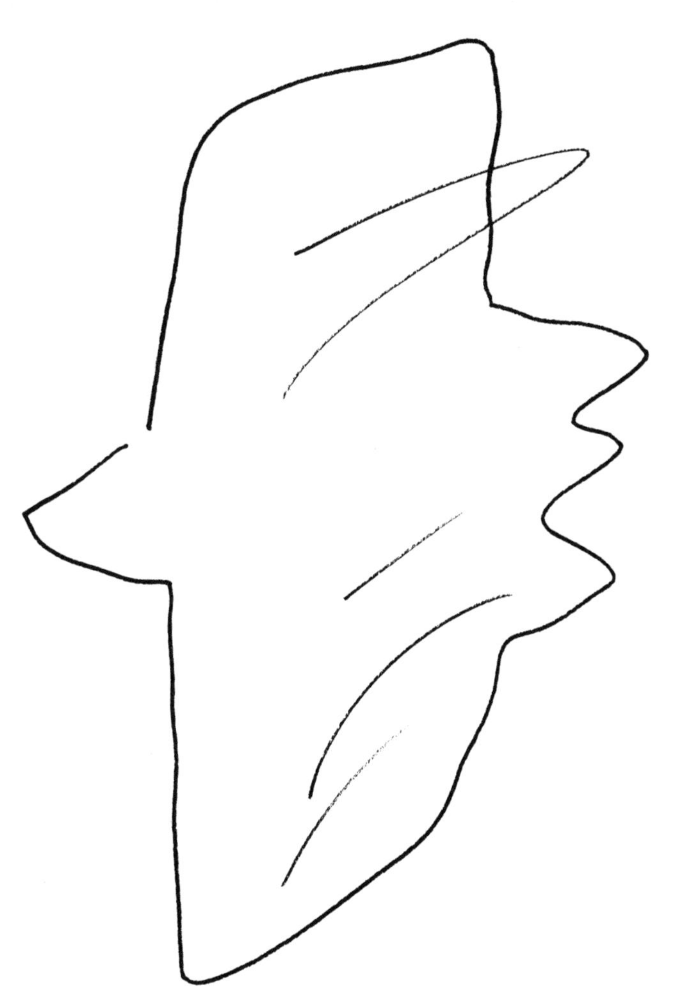

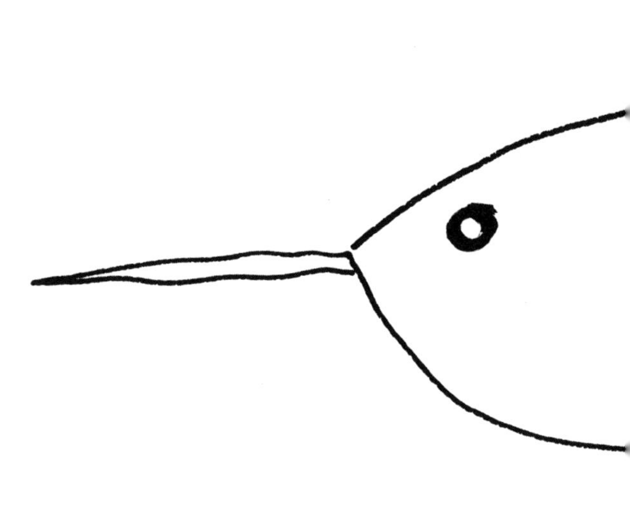

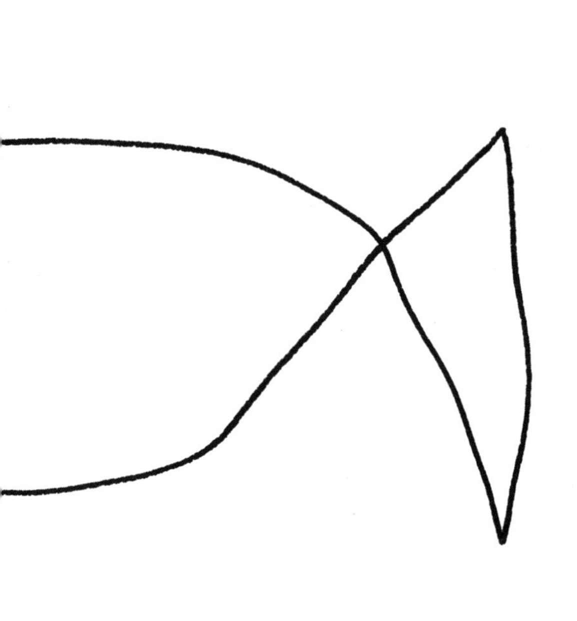

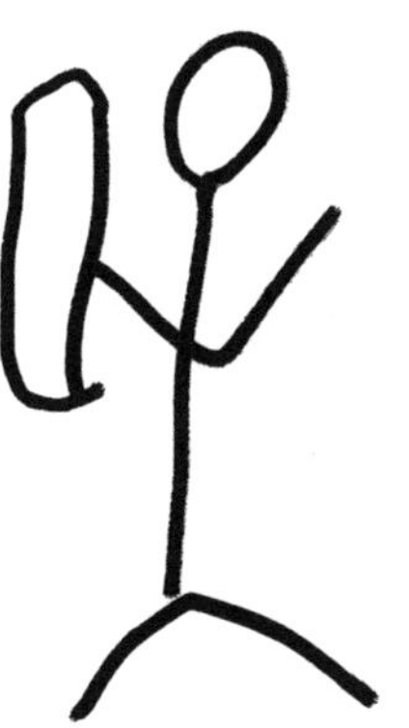

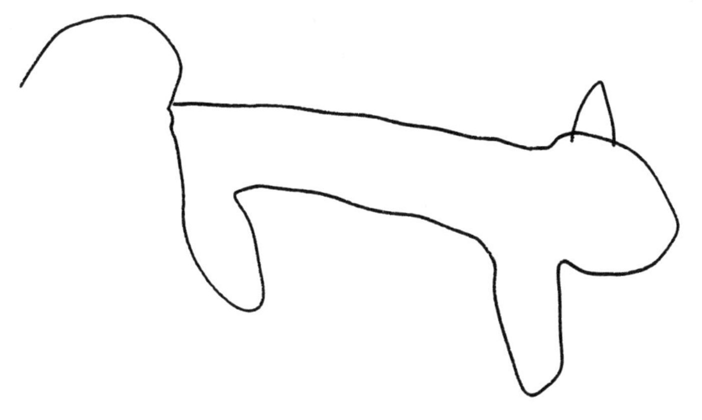

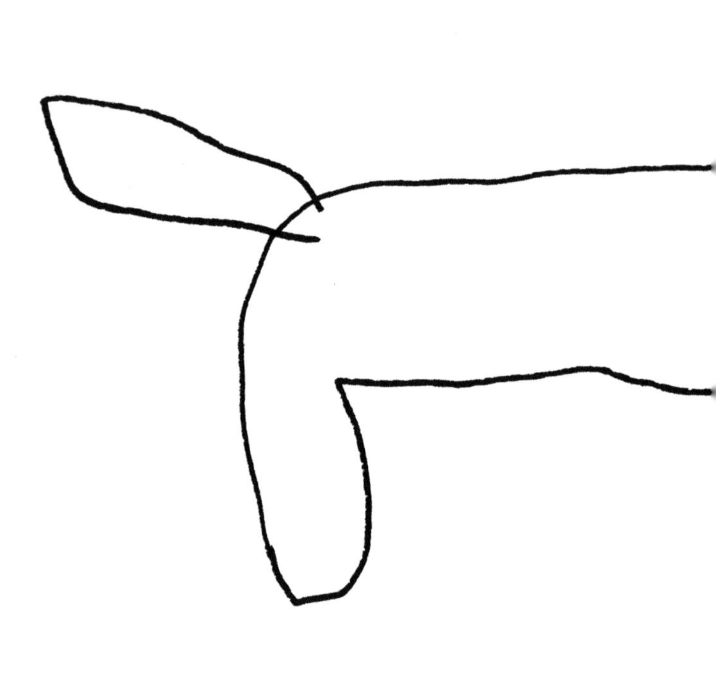

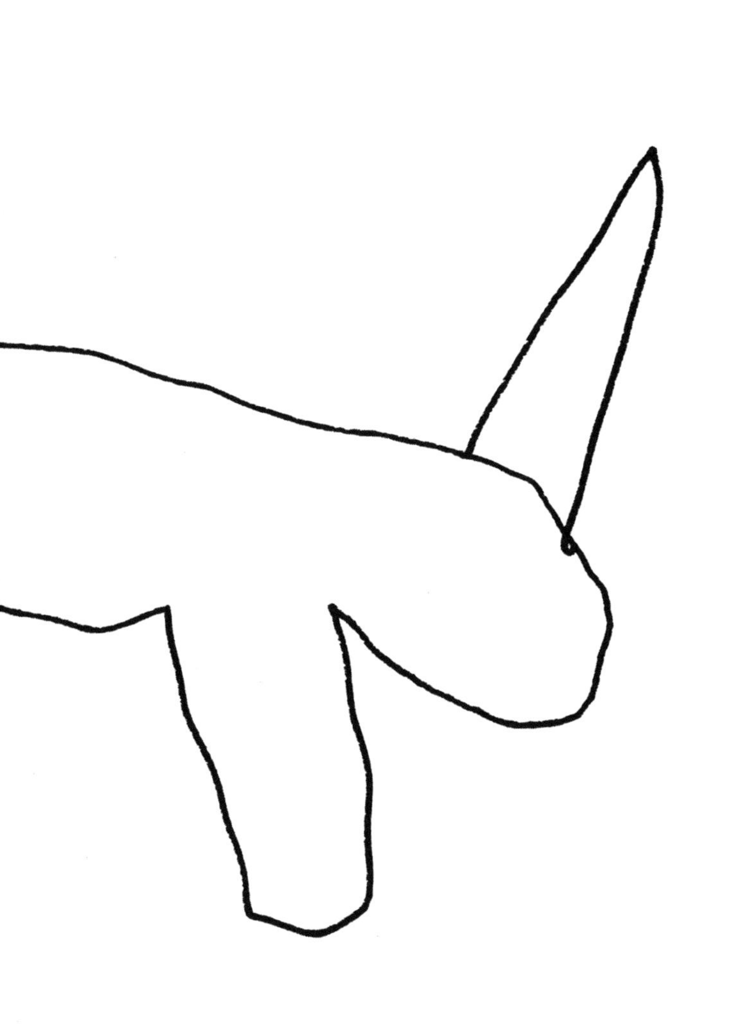

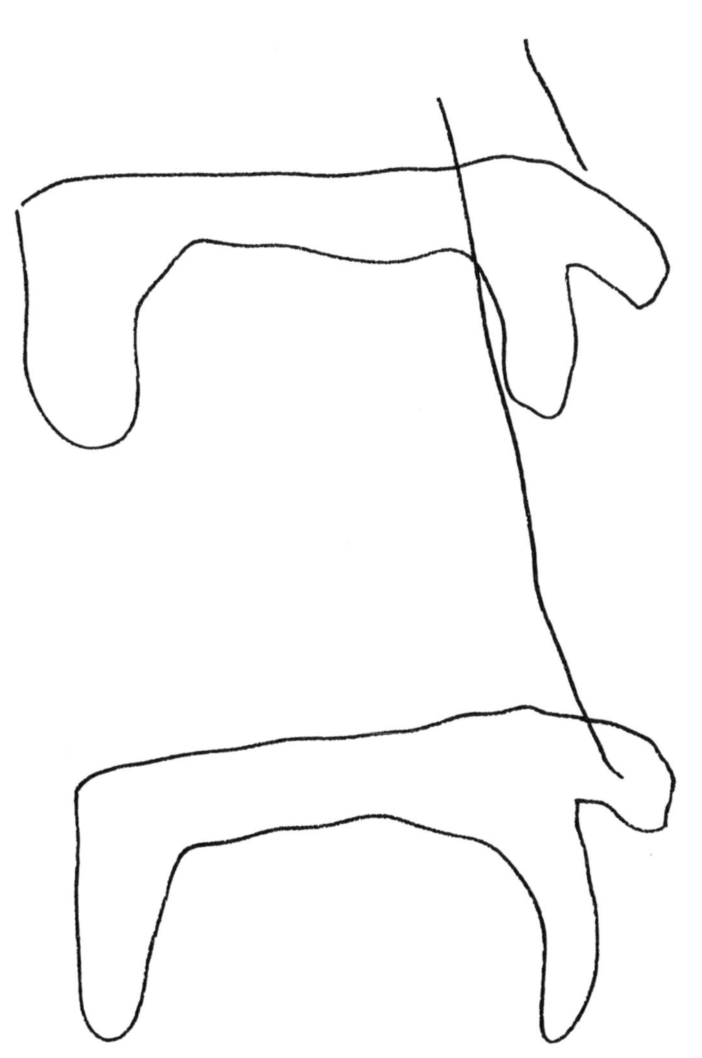

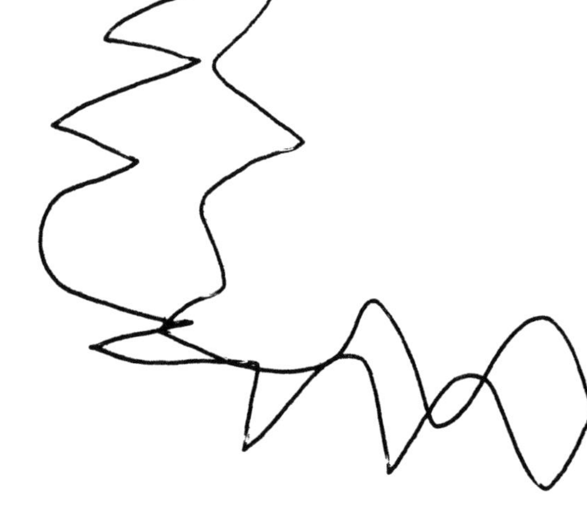

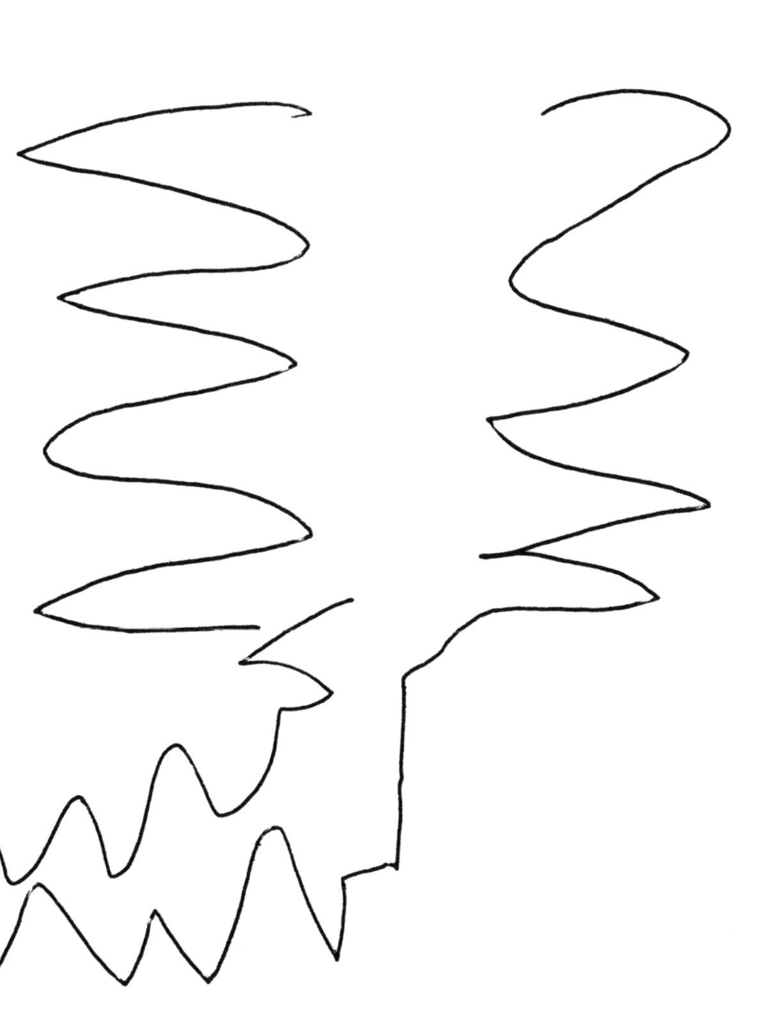

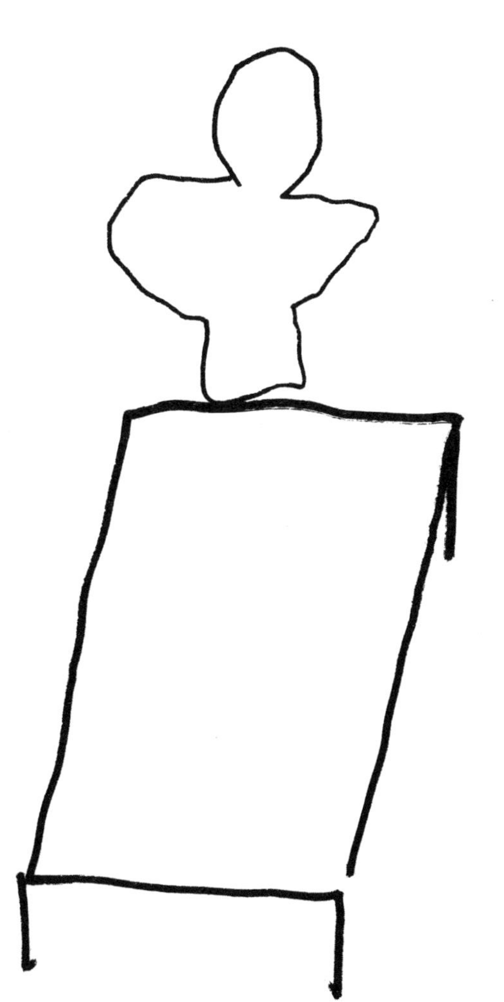

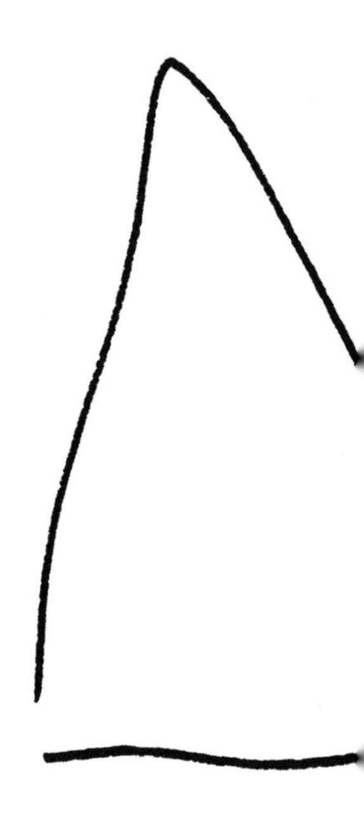

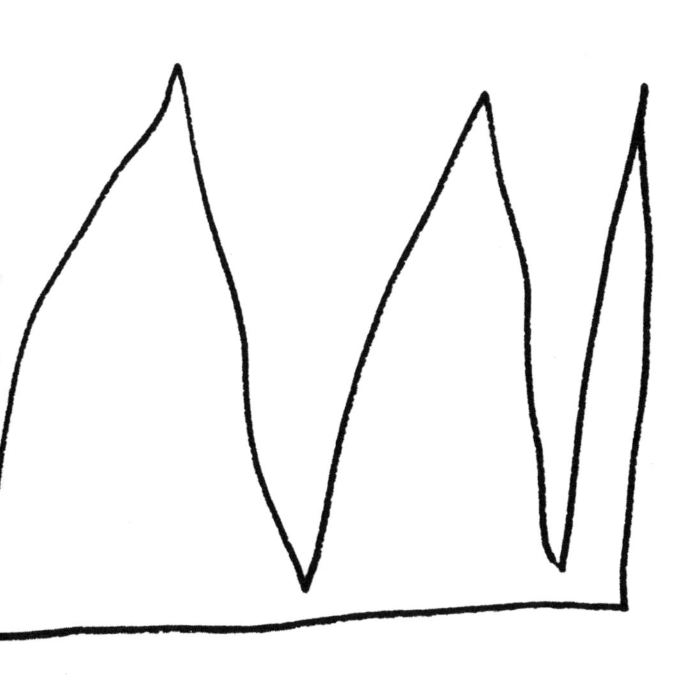

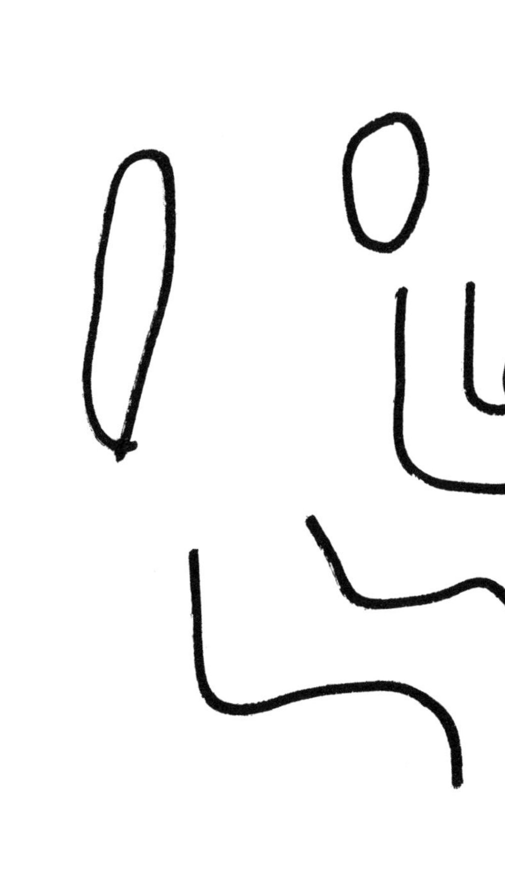

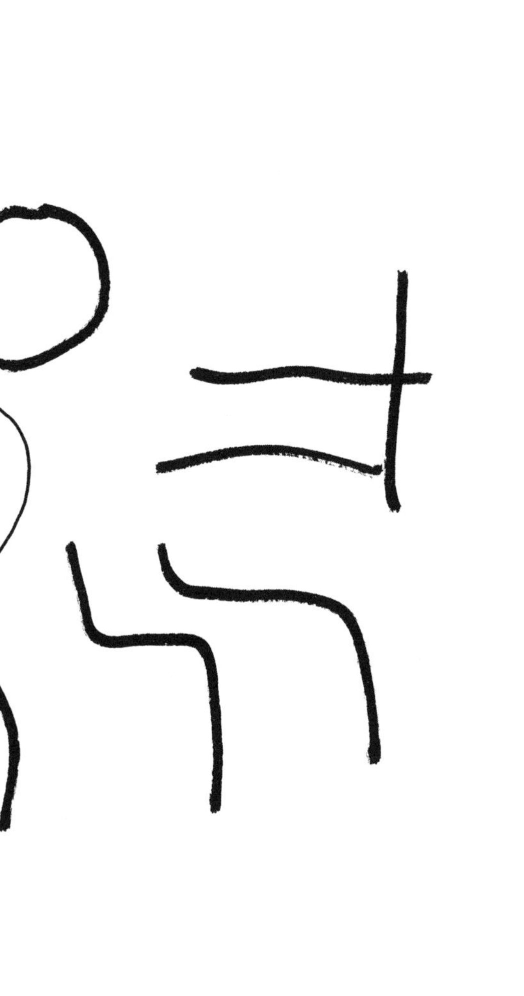

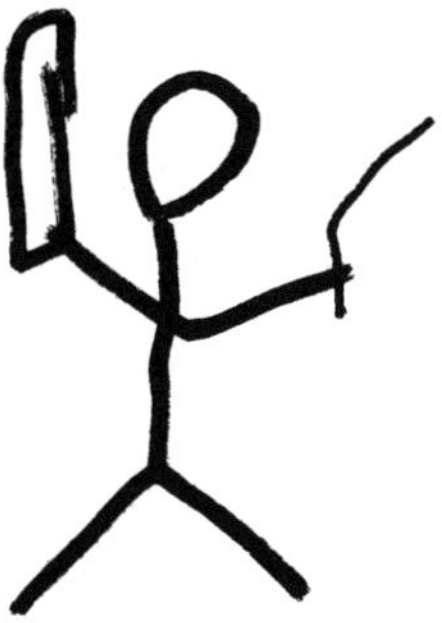

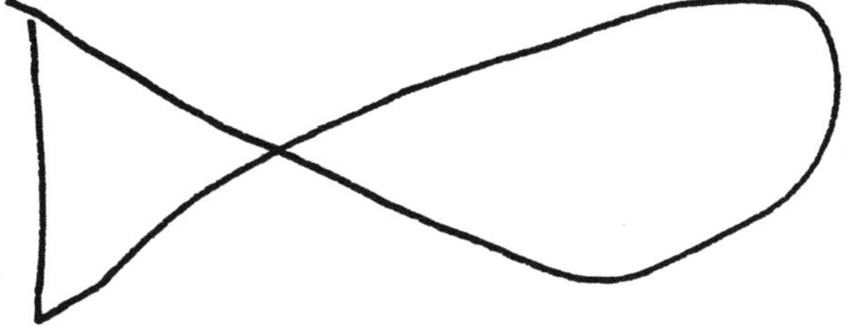

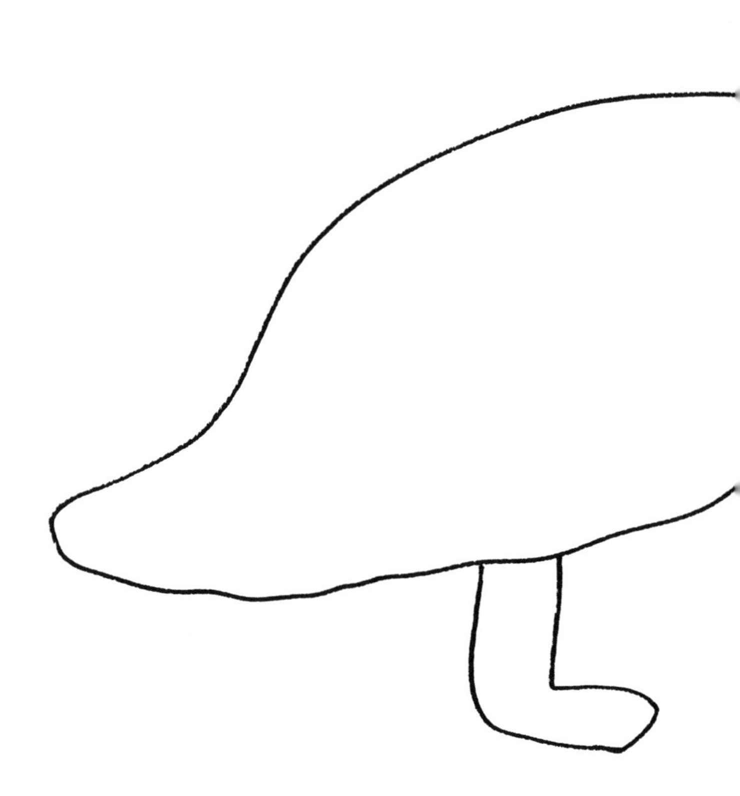

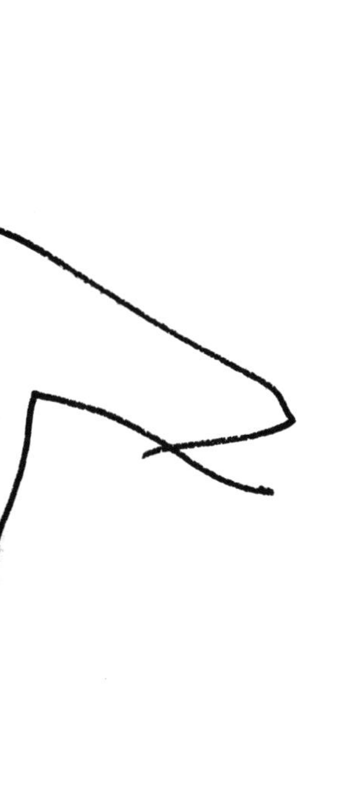

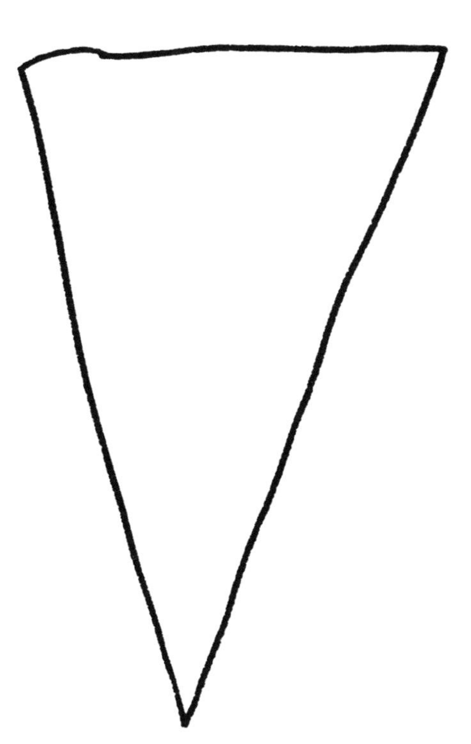

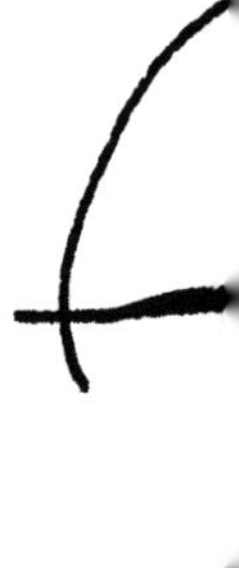

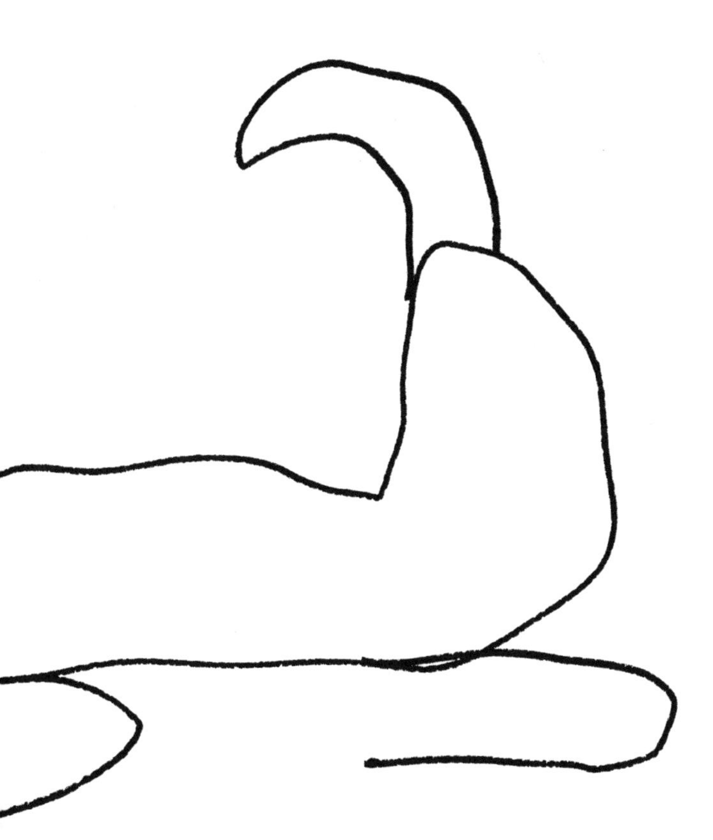

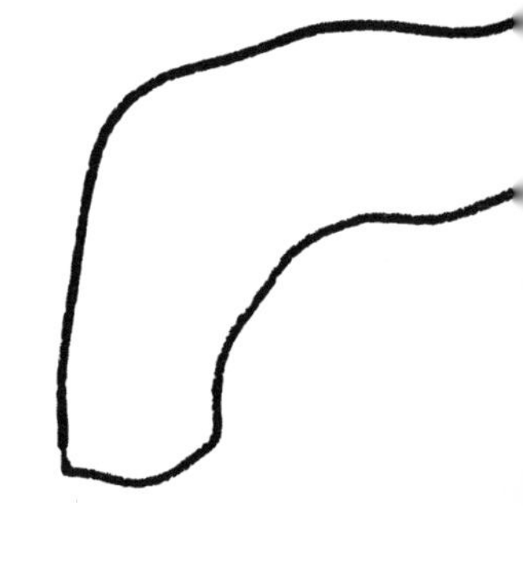

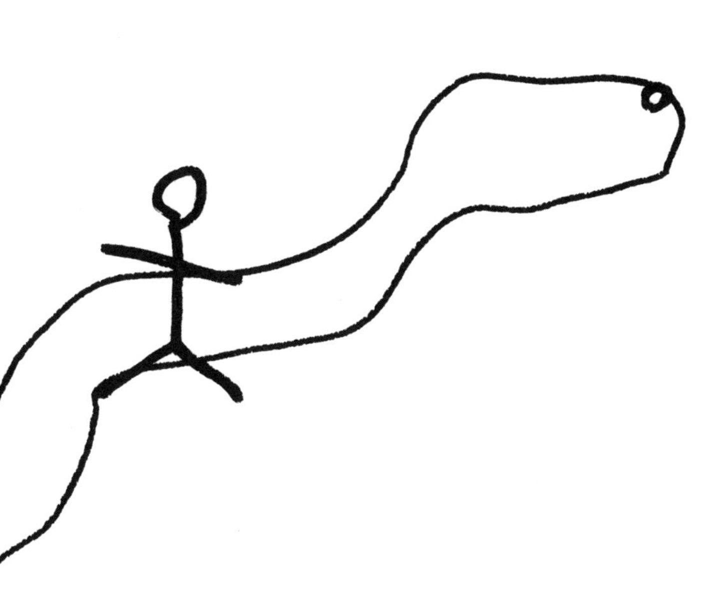

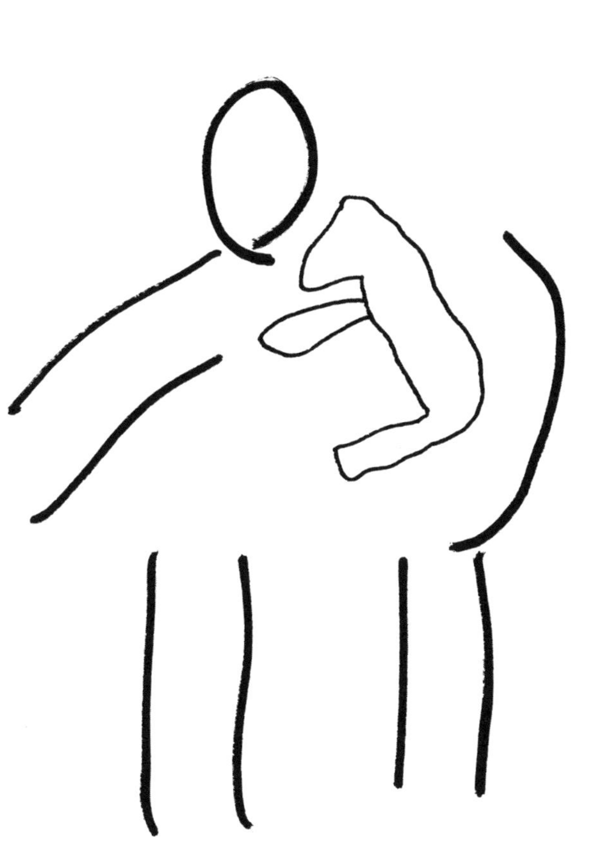

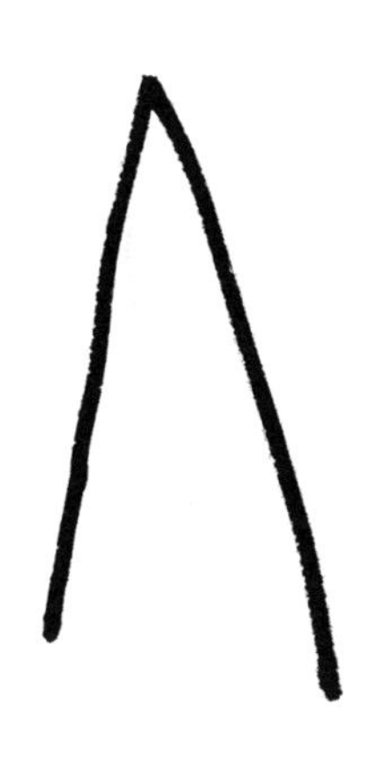

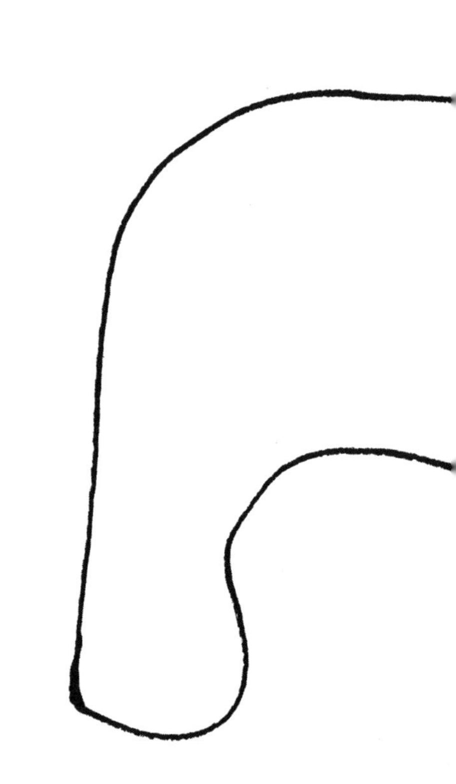

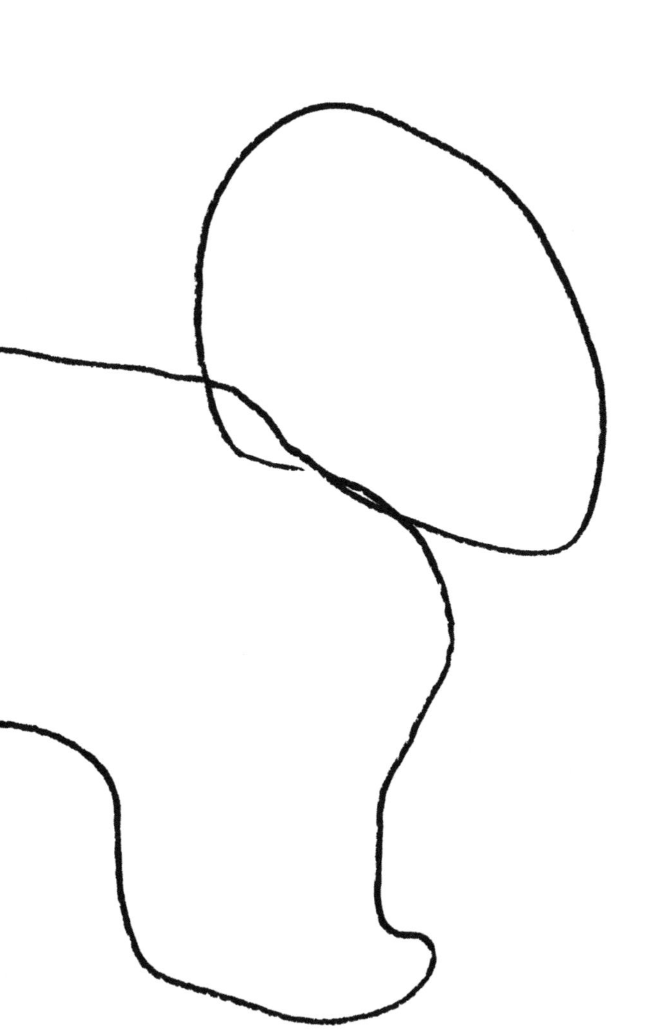

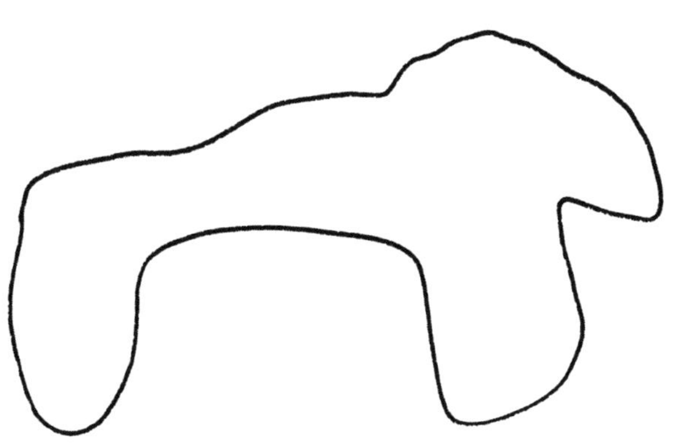

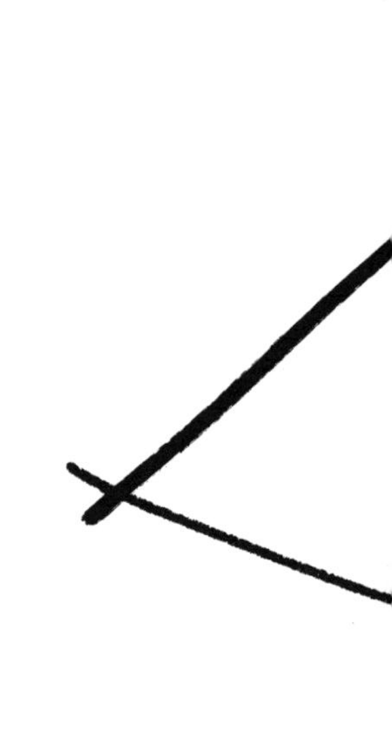

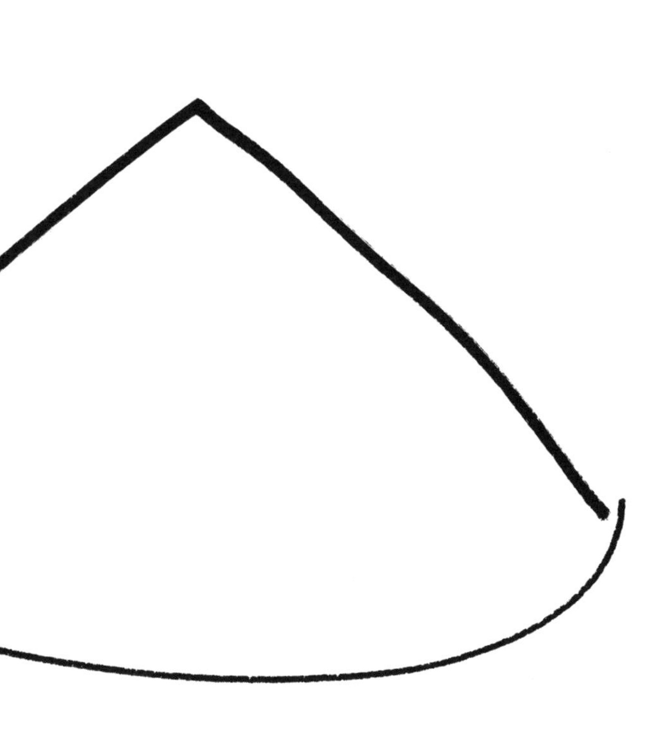

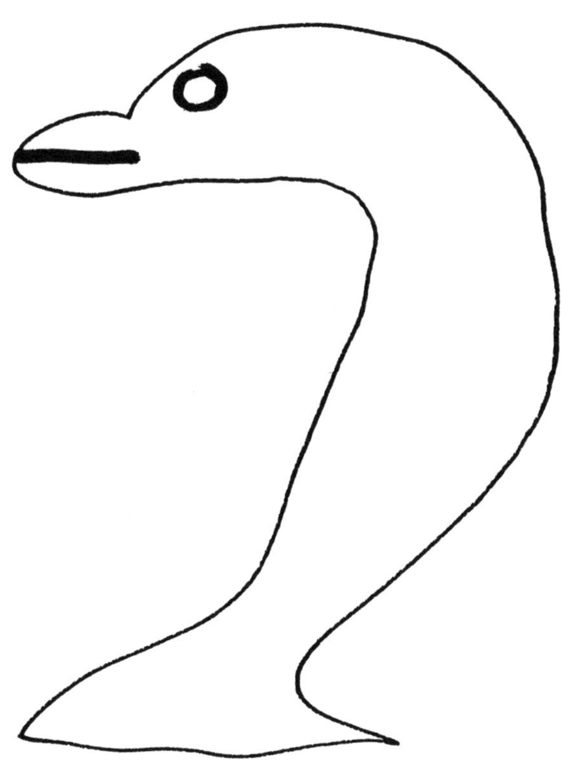

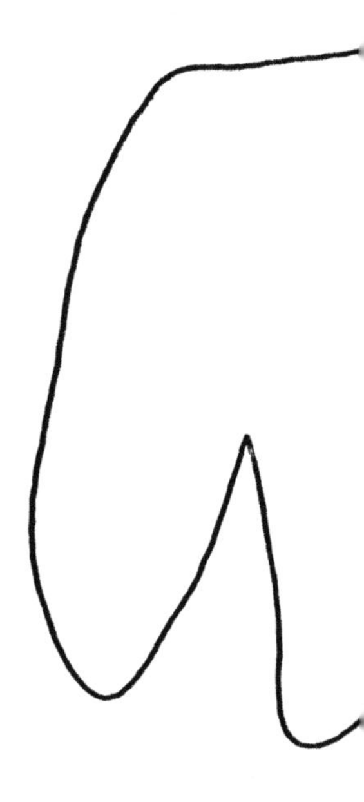

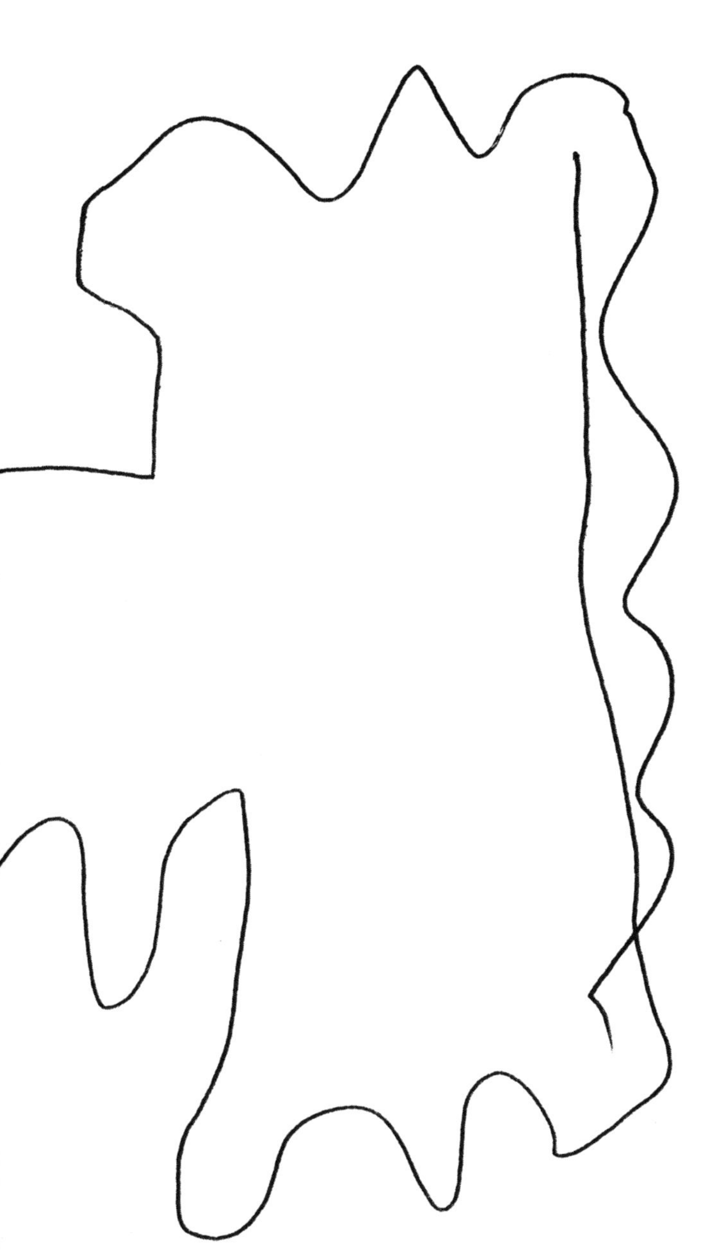

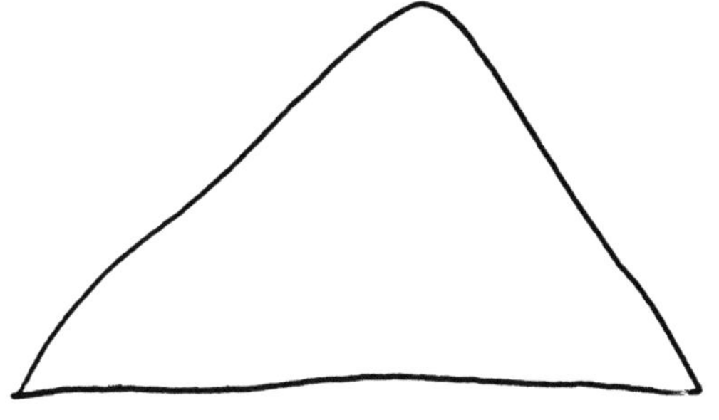

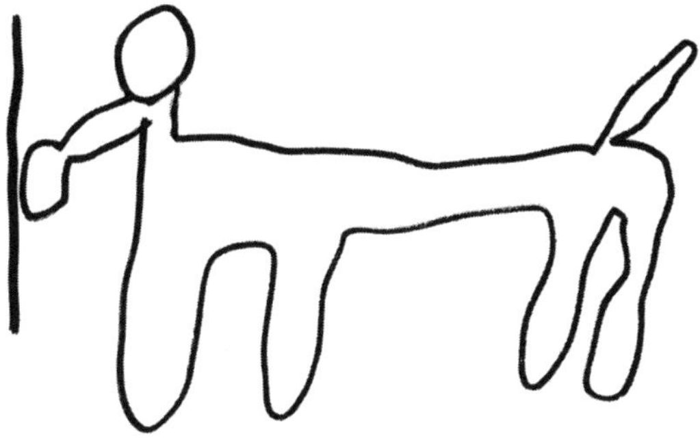

88 Constellations
Index

Cepheus ... 01
Scutum ... 02
Cancer ... 03
Corona Borealis ... 04
Fornax ... 05
Microscopium ... 06
Equuleus ... 07
Sagitta ... 08
Orion ... 09
Pisces ... 10
Horologium ... 11
Draco ... 12
Puppis, Vela & Carina ... 13–15
Pyxis ... 16
Apus ... 17
Aquarius & Piscis Austrinus ... 18–19
Antlia ... 20
Chamaeleon ... 21
Ursa Minor ... 22
Indus ... 23
Camelopardalis ... 24
Ursa Major ... 25
Taurus ... 26
Pictor ... 27
Virgo ... 28
Reticulum ... 29

Cetus   30
Columba   31
Andromeda   32
Musca   33
Pegasus   34
Cygnus   35
Cassiopeia   36
Leo   37
Mensa   38
Norma   39
Libra   40
Pavo   41
Coma Berenices   42
Eridanus   43
Crux   44
Lupus   45
Hydra   46
Crater   47
Sagittarius   48
Canis Major   49
Telescopium   50
Vulpecula   51
Perseus   52
Lyra   53
Tucana   54
Grus   55
Hydrus   56
Lacerta   57
Leo Minor   58

Ara	59
Lepus	60
Caelum	61
Octans	62
Aquila	63
Draco	64
Bootes	65
Lynx	66
Monoceros	67
Canes Venatici	68
Scorpius	69
Sculptor	70
Corona Australis	71
Gemini	72
Hercules	73
Volans	74
Corvus	75
Triangulum	76
Capricornus	77
Serpens & Ophiuchus	78–79
Auriga	80
Circinus	81
Aries	82
Canis Minor	83
Sextans	84
Delphinus	85
Phoenix	86
Triangulum Australe	87
Centaurus	88

Masanao Hirayama
88 Constellations

New Documents (21)
978-1-953441-02-7